MW01713900

Summer Book 4

for students entering fourth grade in the fall

by Angela M. Ankers, M. Ed.
Jodi Yarusinsky

Summerbook Company

ISBN: 978-1-933055-14-5

Printed in the United States of America

Summerbook Company
305 Lyndale Drive
Hartsville, SC 29550
(757) 678-4001
www.summerbookcompany.com

Definitions and Helps

An action verb is a word that shows action.

An adjective is a word that describes a noun.

Antonyms are words that are opposites.

Articles (a, an, the) are considered to be adjectives in this book.

A declarative sentence states something or gives a command.

An exclamatory sentence shows strong feeling or emotion.

Homonyms are words that sound the same but are spelled differently. (hair, hare)

An interrogative sentence asks a question.

A noun is a word that names a person, place, or thing.

Plural means the word is talking about two or more things.

A sentence must have a noun and a verb.

Singular means the word is talking about one of something.

Synonyms are words that mean the same thing. (boy, lad)

A verb is a word that shows action, state of being or helps another verb.

How to Use This Book Effectively

1. Do one page a day in this book. If the page contains something difficult for your child, make sure he understands what he is doing. Do not allow him to guess his way through it. The answer key begins after page 50 for your convenience. You may wish to tear it out and store it in a separate place.

2. Do not become overly concerned if your child has difficulty with several exercises in this book. Reread the directions with him and help him do the first few. If he still does not understand, this may mean that he has already forgotten what he has learned, and he really needs to work on this skill before the new school year begins. It may also mean that the curriculum used last year did not introduce the skill. To decide which of these two reasons is the correct one, look through any old papers you may have. If you do not see any work similar to the exercise, skip all of the same type of exercises in the book, unless you have the patience and desire to teach your child how to do them. Your child cannot "review" things he has never been taught.

3. Be patient and encouraging. It can be difficult to think about letters and numbers when it is sunny outside and a sibling is already playing in the pool.

4. Have your child read regularly, preferably daily. Your local library can provide an abundance of interesting stories for your child. Grade-appropriate books are also available on our website, www.summerbookcompany.com.

Add.

71	54	30	25	99	76	42	92	78	33
+ 49	+ 97	+ 68	+ 83	+ 12	+ 28	+ 46	+ 39	+ 4	+ 91

Subtract to find how much change should be made. Draw coins to show the change.

Randy bought a race car for $4.79. He paid $5.00.	Susan bought a necklace for $3.14. She paid $3.50.
Hannah bought a dozen eggs for $0.67. She paid $1.00.	Joe bought a candy bar for $0.39. He paid $0.50.

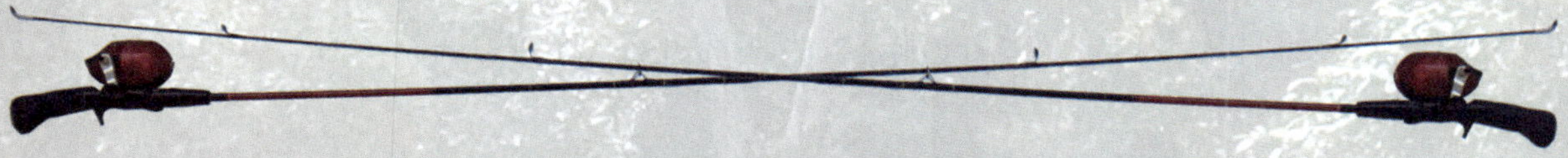

*Put a ✓ over the underlined word if it is a noun. Put an **X** over the word if it is not a noun.*

1. My grandfather and I like to fish from the small dock in his backyard.
2. We often go fishing very early in the morning before the sun gets too hot.
3. Sometimes I accidentally catch a turtle instead of a catfish or a bass.
4. Grandfather helps me put the bait on the hook and take the fish off the hook.

Circle the letters in the story that should be a capital letter.

last july, i went to the mountains for a camping trip. i left on friday afternoon. on saturday, july 4th, i decided to take an extra long hike because it was independence day. i hiked and hiked for several hours. when i got back to my campsite, my friend julie was there. i was surprised to see her. after we ate supper, we roasted marshmallows over the fire. it was a wonderful 4th of july.

Number each group of items in order from least to greatest.

______ year
______ second
______ week
______ minute
______ month
______ hour
______ day

______ inch
______ centimeter
______ yard
______ foot
______ meter
______ mile

______ senior citizen
______ infant
______ adult
______ child
______ teenager
______ toddler

______ larva
______ egg
______ adult
______ pupa

______ city
______ state
______ house
______ street
______ country

______ floor
______ roof
______ foundation
______ walls

______ flour
______ dough
______ wheat
______ bread
______ sandwich

______ sauce
______ crust
______ toppings
______ cheese
______ eating

______ ice cream
______ whipped topping
______ cherry
______ fudge sauce

Tuesday

Multiply.

0	6	8	2	4	10	11	39	75	23
x 9	x 4	x 7	x 3	x 5	x 0	x 6	x 1	x 2	x 8

Color the correct amount on each bar.

0.2	0.1	0.3
0.6	0.4	0.8
0.5	0.9	0.7

Subtract. Do not let the large numbers scare you.

$$\begin{array}{r} 5{,}296{,}473{,}018 \\ -\ \ \ 135{,}262{,}004 \\ \hline \end{array} \qquad \begin{array}{r} 9{,}876{,}543{,}210 \\ -\ \ \ 385{,}124{,}603 \\ \hline \end{array}$$

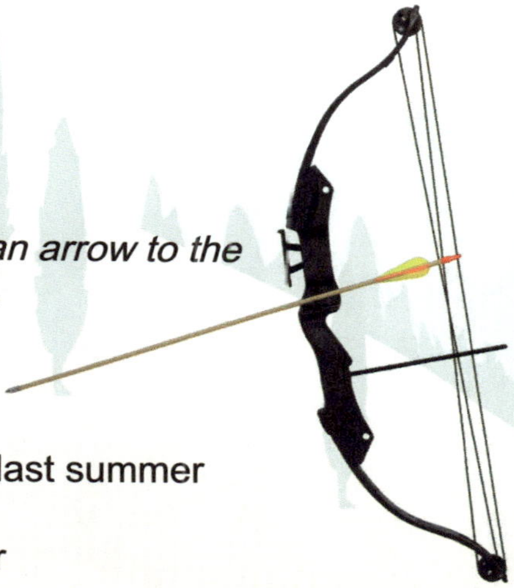

Underline the adjectives in each sentence; then draw an arrow to the word it describes. Put periods where they are needed.

1. Ben has a small bow and several sharp arrows
2. They were a special birthday gift from Uncle Henry last summer
3. Ben shoots at the large target with the yellow center
4. This summer, Ben will be taking archery lessons
5. He wants to compete in the archery contest this fall with three friends

Write the words for which the contraction stands.

can't ______________________ you're ______________________

she's ______________________ won't ______________________

we'll ______________________ I'm ______________________

☺ **Something Extra** ☺

Write a letter to someone in your family like your grandmother or an uncle. See if you can also address the envelope correctly without help!

Find the names of twenty-five states in the puzzle. Be very careful. Some state names have been spelled incorrectly to try to trick you. Only circle the name of each state when it is spelled correctly.

A	L	L	A	B	A	A	R	K	A	N	S	A	S	A	I	M	R
R	S	C	O	N	N	E	C	T	I	C	U	T	M	K	N	A	I
K	G	K	L	A	C	A	L	I	F	O	R	N	I	A	D	R	D
A	I	E	O	H	M	I	C	H	I	G	A	N	M	N	I	Y	A
N	L	N	I	A	M	I	N	N	E	S	O	T	A	S	A	L	H
G	L	T	U	L	D	E	L	A	W	A	R	E	F	E	N	A	O
E	I	U	S	A	M	A	S	S	A	C	H	U	L	S	A	N	A
O	N	C	I	B	M	A	I	N	N	C	O	L	O	R	A	D	O
R	O	K	H	A	W	A	I	I	M	G	M	K	R	M	A	N	E
G	I	Y	C	M	F	M	I	S	S	I	S	S	I	P	P	I	H
I	S	M	K	A	C	H	K	A	N	S	A	S	D	I	W	O	A
A	R	I	Z	O	N	A	F	G	E	O	R	G	A	M	F	M	L
I	O	W	A	O	M	A	S	S	A	C	H	U	S	E	T	T	S
M	F	L	H	C	M	A	I	N	E	D	E	L	A	W	E	A	R
C	O	M	A	L	A	S	K	A	F	M	I	S	S	O	U	R	I
H	A	W	A	A	I	G	L	O	U	I	S	I	A	N	A	K	C

Alabama
Alaska
Arizona
Arkansas
California
Colorado
Connecticut
Delaware
Florida
Georgia
Hawaii
Idaho
Illinois
Indiana
Iowa
Kansas
Kentucky
Louisiana
Maine
Maryland
Massachusetts
Michigan
Minnesota
Mississippi
Missouri

Wednesday

Subtract.

511	832	673	940	724	862	570	793
- 409	- 197	- 85	- 368	- 256	- 337	- 108	- 59

Use the numbers to make four equations.

3 21 7	2 18 9	5 10 2
___ x ___ = ___	___ x ___ = ___	___ x ___ = ___
___ x ___ = ___	___ x ___ = ___	___ x ___ = ___
___ ÷ ___ = ___	___ ÷ ___ = ___	___ ÷ ___ = ___
___ ÷ ___ = ___	___ ÷ ___ = ___	___ ÷ ___ = ___

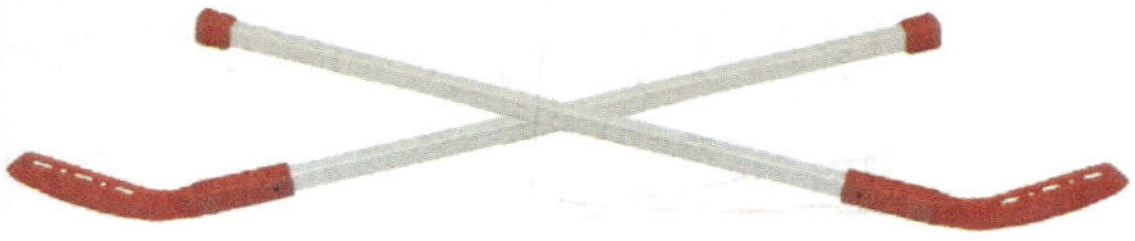

Put the correct punctuation at the end of each sentence. Then tell whether the sentence is **exclamatory**, **declarative** *or* **interrogative**.

____________ 1. The boys on Covington Drive like to play street hockey

____________ 2. Do you know when the next game will be

____________ 3. The boys usually play on George's large, long driveway

____________ 4. Yeah! Peter scored a goal

____________ 5. Have you ever played street hockey

Place commas in the sentences.

1. Yes Kendra you may go to the party.
2. The President lives in Washington D. C.
3. No Mr. Hankins is not in his office right now.
4. John would you please close the door?
5. Thomas Edison's research laboratory was built in Menlo Park New Jersey.

☞ **Try This!** ☜

Take an empty plastic milk jug and rinse it with HOT water until the jug is hot all over. Now pour out the water and put the cap on tightly. Set it in the freezer and wait 20 minutes. Can you explain what happened?

Fill in each blank with the best word from the bottom of the page.

George Washington was a great man, not because he was our first ____________________, but because he was an honest man and tried to do ___________ every day.

He knew that it is better to think of others before we think about _____________________. When George Washington was young, he listed rules for good ________________________ in a notebook and tried very carefully to live by them. He always treated others and did each job, great or small, to the best of his ability. Surveyor, planter, soldier, burgess, delegate or President, he worked ______________ and did each job well.

At his death, the entire nation ______________________. His character and testimony have been ____________________ and respected for many years. In Washington D. C. the

____

was built in memory of his life and leadership. The state of Washington was named after _____________________, and his picture is on the Washington state ________________.

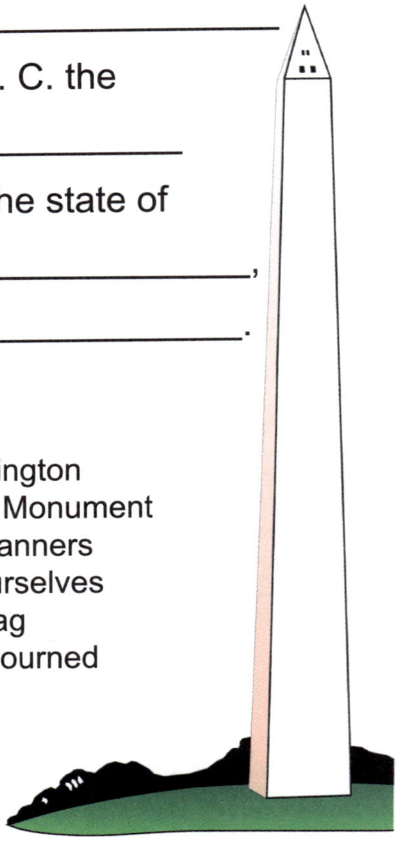

President Washington
Washington National Monument

honored	manners
courteously	ourselves
President	flag
diligently	mourned
right	

Thursday

Divide.

16 ÷ 8 = _____	20 ÷ 4 = _____	2 ÷ 1 = _____	42 ÷ 6 = _____
9 ÷ 3 = _____	16 ÷ 2 = _____	28 ÷ 7 = _____	0 ÷ 5 = _____
54 ÷ 9 = _____	2 ÷ 2 = _____	45 ÷ 9 = _____	12 ÷ 2 = _____

Add.

34	391	89	95	177	53	11	425
72	247	65	42	121	84	45	274
+ 58	+ 423	+ 16	+ 28	+ 536	+ 69	+ 97	+ 351

Write the plural form of the words on the lines.

city ____________	glass ____________	tree ____________
bench ____________	daddy ____________	leaf ____________
cat ____________	church ____________	copy ____________
knife ____________	ball ____________	class ____________

Number the words in each column in alphabetical order.

____ bear	____ Joseph	____ Rachel	____ maple
____ lion	____ Nathan	____ Sarah	____ oak
____ bird	____ James	____ Alice	____ pine
____ frog	____ Peter	____ Susan	____ aspen
____ lamb	____ Doug	____ Angela	____ apple

Circle the correct word.

1. Don't eat (to, two, too) much candy before the game or you will feel sick.
2. I am going (to, two, too) learn (to, two, too) juggle more than (to, too, two) clubs.
3. Juggling is not (to, too, two) hard if a person will practice a lot.
4. At the circus, (to, too, two) men juggled clubs (together, toogether).

Hint Hunter

Hint Hunter pages are a chance for you to use your brain to figure out something that you have never been told. Here is an example:

Heather, Helen, and Hannah each have a different pet. Heather keeps her pet in a glass bowl on her dresser. Hannah walks her pet every day. Circle the pet that belongs to each girl.

Now think about what you just read. Which would you keep in a glass bowl? A dog? No. A goldfish may be kept in a glass bowl. So Heather has a goldfish, and the other two girls do not. Circle Heather's goldfish and put an X on the other two fish. You can also put X's on the parakeet and the dog in Heather's row because she only has one pet.

Now, which pet would you take for a walk? A dog, so circle Hannah's dog and put an X on the other dogs. You can also put an X on the other pets in Hannah's row. Which pet is left for Helen? The parakeet.

When you are done, your paper should look like this.

Now you try this one.

Four boys went to the sporting goods store and bought something different. Carl plans to use what he bought when he is in the basement with his dad. Adam did not buy a ball. Bobby's purchase was round. What did each boy buy?

In what place is the seven?

75 <u>tens</u>	4726 ______	7 ______
607 ______	5397 ______	67,253 ______
7426 ______	79 ______	979 ______

Solve the story problems.

1. Alston Classical School has 215 in the elementary school and 117 in the high school. How many students do they have altogether?

____

2. Mrs. Burns makes aprons. She can make two aprons from one yard of material. If she has ten yards of blue material, how many aprons can she make?

____

3. Doug bought a race car for $2.37 and a dump truck for $2.69. If he gave the clerk $6.00, how much change should he receive?

____

4. Monica wanted to share her bag of 12 cookies fairly with her 3 friends. How many cookies should she give to each person? (Monica also plans to eat cookies.)

____

Put the quotation marks where they belong in the paragraph.

Jenna, do you want to play volleyball? asked Teresa. We bought a new net yesterday.

Sure, said Jenna. That sounds like fun. Let's ask Mary and Ginger to join us.

I'll go ask Mary while you ask Ginger, offered Teresa. I'll meet you in my backyard in a couple of minutes.

Underline the subject(s) once and the verb(s) twice.

1. The horses galloped and chased each other around the pasture.
2. It is warm and sunny outside today.
3. The car swerved around the sharp corner.
4. The lightning flashed and the thunder crashed.
5. The dictionary is a great big book.

The Gnat and the Lion
Aesop

A gnat once went up to a lion and said, “I am not in the least afraid of you. I don’t even think that you are a match for me in strength. What does your strength amount to after all? You can scratch with your claws and bite with your teeth and nothing more. But I am stronger than you. If you don’t believe it, let us fight and see.”

So saying, the gnat sounded his horn, and darted in and bit the lion on the nose. When the lion felt the sting, in his haste to crush him, he scratched his nose badly and made it bleed. But he did not hurt the gnat at all.

The gnat buzzed off in triumph, happy about his victory. Presently, however, he was caught in a spider’s web and was eaten by the spider. Thus, he fell prey to an insignificant creature after having triumphed over the King of the Beasts.

Answer the questions about the story.

1. Which animal was bragging? gnat lion spider
2. Circle the antonym for *haste*. hurry slow hate
3. Write a homonym for *prey*. ________________
4. What is the moral of this story?______________

____

____

____

____

____

____

Monday

Add.

\$2.84	\$5.17	349	\$1.37	\$3.15	245	\$5.68
+ .56	+ 1.75	+ 408	+ .66	+ .98	+ 424	+ .26

Use the numbers to make four math facts.

7 9 2	8 12 4	6 10 4
____ + ____ = ____	____ + ____ = ____	____ + ____ = ____
____ + ____ = ____	____ + ____ = ____	____ + ____ = ____
____ - ____ = ____	____ - ____ = ____	____ - ____ = ____
____ - ____ = ____	____ - ____ = ____	____ - ____ = ____

In what place is the five?

524 hundreds 500,713 ________ 98,650 ________

657,902 ________ 25,391 ________ 405 ________

Write a noun on each blank to make a good story.

I have a pet named ____________. He is lots of fun. I like to play ____________ with him. His favorite toy is a ____________. At night, he sleeps in my ____________. My pet has soft ____________. He especially likes me to rub his ____________. Don't you wish you had a ____________ like mine?

Circle the letters that should be capitalized.

1. i received a new unicycle for christmas.
2. uncle stephen tried to teach me to ride it.
3. on saturday dad is going to try to help me again.
4. i am sure i will love it once i learn how to ride it.
5. grandpa and grandma will be here for thanksgiving and i want to ride it well in front of them.

Choose the operation or operations you would need to do to find the answer. You do not have to solve the problems.

Belinda's Balloon Boutique

Bright balloon bunches--a bargain!

1. Belinda sells a dozen balloons for $17.40. How much is she charging per balloon?

add subtract multiply divide

2. Belinda is having a special. When you buy two big balloons for $2.15 each, the third one is free. How much would six balloons cost during the special?

add subtract multiply divide

3. Arnold's Accounting Service is giving a big retirement party to Mr. Tilgore who has worked there for over thirty years. They are decorating with four dozen balloons that cost $17.40 per dozen and one special retirement balloon that costs $4.75. How much are they going to spend on balloons?

Step 1: add subtract multiply divide

Step 2: add subtract multiply divide

4. Belinda usually keeps thirty-six balloons inflated to decorate the store. This morning when she arrived, she noticed she only had twenty-seven. How many more balloons does she need?

add subtract
multiply divide

5. Usually Belinda's store is very busy and she sells six hundred fifty balloons each week. Last week Belinda sold one thousand balloons. How many extra balloons did she sell last week?

add subtract multiply divide

6. Henry bought one big balloon for $2.15 and a small balloon for $1.25. How much was his total?

add subtract multiply divide

7. Three friends agreed to split the cost of the balloons for their other friend's surprise birthday party. They decided to get a dozen balloons for $17.40, a special birthday balloon for $3.50, and a balloon with a big ten on it for $2.80. How much did each girl have to pay?

Step 1:
add subtract multiply divide

Step 2:
add subtract multiply divide

Optional
For extra practice, go ahead and solve each problem.

Multiply.

7 x 10 = _____	1 x 1 = _____	7 x 3 = _____	2 x 5 = _____
9 x 9 = _____	5 x 7 = _____	10 x 4 = _____	8 x 6 = _____
6 x 0 = _____	4 x 8 = _____	0 x 2 = _____	3 x 10 = _____

Write the correct fraction.

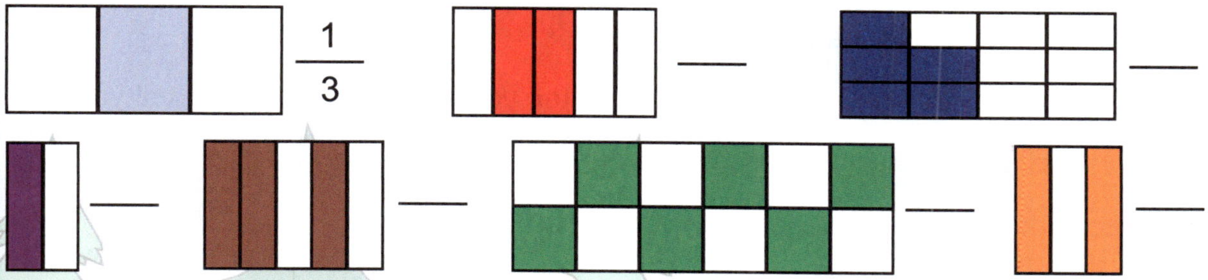

Circle the adjectives in the sentences.

1. My mother grows red tulips, yellow daffodils and purple crocuses in her yard.
2. Dick found a bright, shiny penny in the wet grass.
3. The black, hairy spider crawled up the brick wall.
4. Derek enjoyed the crispy, crunchy cookies.
5. He has a yellow marble, a short string and a green frog in his pockets.

Put periods where they belong in the story.

Last weekend Mr T J Landing went camping on Mt Misty He invited his friend, James S Thomas, to go with him The two men set up camp Then they hiked to old Ft Lookout When they got back, they fixed a big supper and went to bed A few hours later the men heard strange noises What do you think they saw when they looked out of the tent?

Circle the correct word.

1. The teacher (taught, learned) the class how to divide.
2. The boys (taught, learned) how to bait a hook.
3. Will you please (teach, learn) me how to build a fire?

A Quiet Talk with the Looking Glass
from *Childhood's Happy Hours*

If a mirror could speak, what strange things it would say. Some things we might not like to hear. It might say to Agnes, "Aggie, you are a good girl, but you spend too much time looking at me." Or to Robert, "Bob, there is no reason for you to go rushing around in such a hurry. You go to school without even looking at me. Your hair looks as if it had not been brushed for a week."

But suppose the looking glass could tell you its history. It might tell you about its birth and growth, its travel in other lands, the people it has met and the treatment it has received. What a strange story it would be!

Write a story as if you were a mirror and were telling someone your history.

Subtract.

\$53.79	2460	2897	\$42.18	9514	7256
- 4.86	- 501	- 613	- 3.70	- 803	- 931

Put **<** *or* **>** *in the circle.*

9 + 9 ◯ 3 x 3	2 + 7 ◯ 3 + 7	4 x 9 ◯ 8 x 4	3 x 5 ◯ 6 + 5
6 + 7 ◯ 4 x 0	8 + 5 ◯ 0 + 9	9 x 5 ◯ 1 x 8	8 x 1 ◯ 4 + 7
1 + 6 ◯ 5 x 4	8 + 6 ◯ 1 + 2	2 x 4 ◯ 5 x 6	1 x 6 ◯ 1 + 3

Fill in the temperatures.

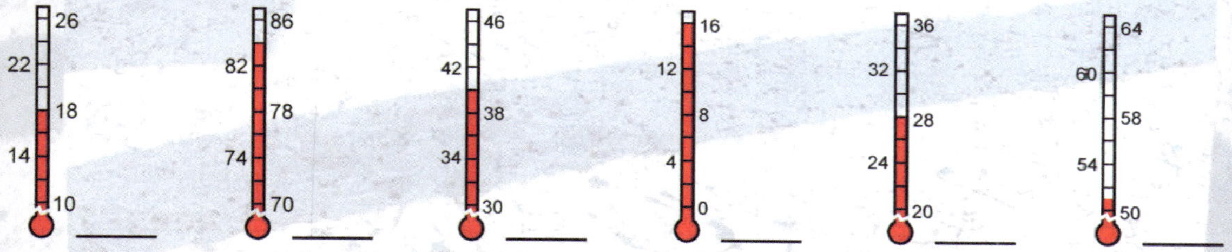

Use **he**, **she**, *or* **it** *in the sentences.*

1. Benjamin thinks __________ is fun to slide down the slide.
2. Sarah is very little; __________ is afraid to go down the slide.
3. I think __________ is fun to slide with my eyes closed.
4. David tried to climb up the slide, but __________ could not.
5. Susan likes the slide, but __________ thinks the swings are the best.

Put commas where they belong.

1. Mother bought milk eggs bread and soup at the grocery store this morning.
2. On July 4 1776 our country became a separate nation.
3. No Bethany you may not have six cookies for dessert.
4. The long brown snake slithered quietly through the tall green weeds.
5. George Washington was born on February 22 1732 in Westmoreland Virginia.

?? Can They Guess ??

Use the back of this page to write a description of one of your friends, but do not use his or her name. After you are finished, read it to someone and see if they can figure out who it is.

Cross out the item in each row that does not belong. Then tell why the other items belong together.

Example: banana ~~broccoli~~ apple pear
Why? *The other items are all fruits.*

1. Steven Sam Sandra Saul Scott

   Why? ____________________

2. whale shark giraffe bear raccoon

   Why? ____________________

3. monitor mouse radio keyboard speakers

   Why? ____________________

4. Army Navy Air Force Marines soldier Coast Guard

   Why? ____________________

5. ash elm fir ivy oak

   Why? ____________________

6. hamburger jello meatloaf tacos barbecue

   Why? ____________________

7. table chair sofa couch bench

   Why? ____________________

8. cricket ant butterfly roach spider

   Why? ____________________

9. President Mayor Governor Doctor Senator

   Why? ____________________

10. lamp flashlight candle fire tent

    Why? ____________________

Divide.

$6\overline{)36}$	$9\overline{)27}$	$8\overline{)72}$	$7\overline{)0}$	$1\overline{)4}$	$4\overline{)32}$
$4\overline{)16}$	$6\overline{)18}$	$5\overline{)10}$	$8\overline{)40}$	$3\overline{)3}$	$3\overline{)21}$

Fill in the blanks. Remember: 12 inches=1 foot, 3 feet=1 yard

24 inches = _____ feet 9 feet = _____ yards 6 feet = _____ yards

2 yards = _____ feet 36 inches = _____ feet 2 feet = _____ inches

3 feet = _____ inches 3 yards = _____ feet 36 inches = _____ yard

Write **yes** *on the line if the words make a complete sentence. Write* **no** *if they do not make a complete sentence.*

_________ 1. A very long kick in between the goal posts.

_________ 2. The receiver caught the ball.

_________ 3. Dark blue jerseys and bright yellow pants.

_________ 4. The thick green grass and white lines of the field.

_________ 5. The Tigers scored fourteen points in the first half.

Make the bold word plural and write it on the line to finish the sentence.

elf 1. Have you ever read the story about the shoe maker and the ___________?

lady 2. Many ______________ like to go shopping.

box 3. Mrs. Smith carefully packed everything in large ______________.

thief 4. The police caught the _______________ who tried to rob the bank.

shoe 5. Sam, I think your black ______________ would look good with that suit.

Circle the word that is misspelled and write it correctly on the line.

1.	whitch	where	whenever	whose	______________________
2.	necklace	bracelet	earrings	jewlry	______________________
3.	width	hieght	depth	length	______________________
4.	grocery	laundry	libary	hardware	______________________
5.	mistake	mispell	misbehave	mischief	______________________
6.	principel	teacher	librarian	secretary	______________________
7.	twenty	thirty	fourty	fifty	______________________
8.	about	around	untill	later	______________________
9.	unusual	different	strange	wierd	______________________
10.	finish	finaly	completely	done	______________________
11.	calves	intestine	stomach	tounge	______________________
12.	becuse	through	also	though	______________________

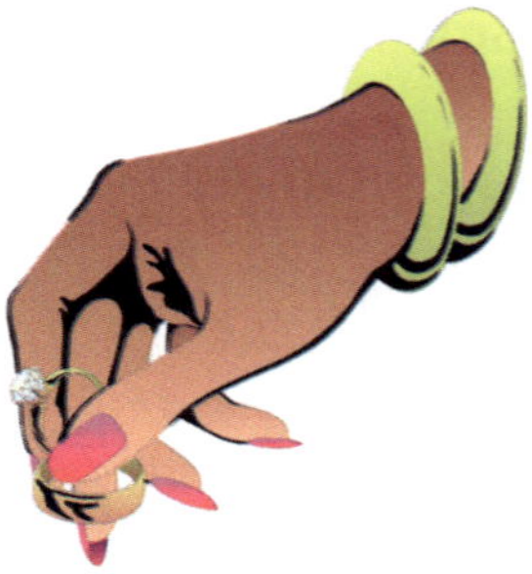

Friday

Fill in the missing numbers.

6 + _____ = 11	6 x _____ = 48	9 + _____ = 16	7 x _____ = 35
5 + _____ = 14	8 x _____ = 64	5 + _____ = 12	5 x _____ = 30
7 + _____ = 14	9 x _____ = 81	8 + _____ = 14	9 x _____ = 54

Solve these story problems.

1. Julie and Jan are saving money to buy a present for their dad. Together they have saved $3.75. They need $9.50. How much more do they need?

____

2. Mr. Bates made 47 signs at work last week, and his partner made 28 signs. How many signs did they make altogether?

____

3. Grandpa's jalopy gets 12 miles per gallon. How far can he travel on 5 gallons of gas?

____

4. At Parker's part-time job he makes $7.00 on Tuesday and $9.00 on Thursday. How much does he make in 4 weeks?

____

*Tell whether the pairs of words are synonyms (**syn.**), homonyms (**hom.**) or antonyms (**ant.**).*

deer, dear ___________	up, down ___________	glad, happy ___________
hot, cold ___________	eight, ate ___________	large, big ___________
pear, pair ___________	near, close ___________	yes, no ___________
boy, lad ___________	stop, go ___________	meet, meat ___________

Circle the correct word.

1. (They're, Their, There) letting us stay with them at the beach.
2. Will you please spread out the towels over (they're, their, there)?
3. I love to play at the beach when (its it's) sunny.
4. Did Susan help mother (set, sit) out the picnic lunch?
5. The wind (blew, blue) the water into big waves.

At West Point
from *Our Hero General U.S. Grant*

It was in the year 1839 that Grant went to West Point. West Point is a school where the drill is the same year in and year out. Young men are sent there from all parts of the United States to learn the art of war.

Ulysses did not need to be taught how to mount or to ride a horse. He knew all that. He made friends there who were good friends until the day of his death. These friends knew that he tried to do what was right, just and true and had a clear head and a pure mind.

He did not talk much, but he was as fond of fun as most boys are. It had to be the right kind of fun or he would not take part in it. He did not swear. He did not want to hear bad jokes, which is more than can be said of most men.

This one thing shows how brave Grant was at this time. He was firm to stick to what he thought was the right course. He had set out to be a good man and a clean man. God gave him strength to turn from all that was bad and to live so that he would not have to blush with shame for his past deeds. He could not have known then how high he was to stand in the eyes of the world. He did not know how each act of his life would be brought and held up to view in the clear light of fame.

Answer the questions about General Grant.

1. What is West Point? a school a battle a man

2. Using two or three complete sentences, describe General Grant's character while he was at West Point.

____

____

____

____

____

Add.

395	269	405	156	370	543	484	502
+ 532	+ 152	+ 211	+ 63	+ 426	+ 120	+ 250	+ 440

Subtract to find how much change should be made. Draw coins to show the change.

Mrs. Neal bought a tomato plant for $2.43. She paid $3.00.	Mr. Bill bought a shovel for $5.82. He paid $6.00.
Mr. Lucas bought some fertilizer for $9.22. He paid $9.25.	Miss Spring bought some tulips for $3.17. She paid $3.25.

Put capital letters where they belong. Cross out any that do not belong.

Have you ever Read *one morning in maine*? it is a Cute story about a little girl named sal who lost her Tooth. the Tooth not only fell out of her mouth but also got lost before she could Put it under her pillow. sal tried To wish on a feather to see if she could still get her wish. you should read the Book to see what happened.

Circle all the nouns in the following sentences.

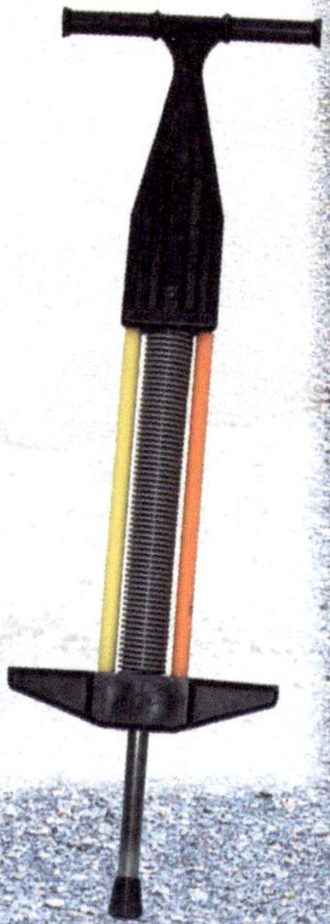

1. Sarah has a pogo stick that she shares with Francis.
2. The girls like to hop down the driveway like a kangaroo.
3. Sarah fell off quite a bit, but she continued to practice.
4. Occasionally the girls have a bouncing contest to see who can hop the most times.
5. Sarah also shares the pogo stick with her brother and his friends.

Answer the questions about the map.

1. Ohio Avenue is between what other two Avenues?

    ______________________ ______________________

2. The north end of Little Drive meets what street?

    ____

3. The south end of Broad Street touches the corner of what two streets?

    ______________________ ______________________

4. Which end of Short Lane is closest to Idaho Avenue?

    ____

5. What street is south of Main Street? ______________________

6. How many roads does Ohio Avenue cross? ______________________

7. The town bank is at the south end of Little Drive. Put a $ at the bank's location.

8. The Vernons live on the north side of Main Street between Maine Avenue and Ohio Avenue. Put a ◊ where their house would be.

9. The new playground is being built on the west end of Narrow Way on the north side of the street. Put a ☺ where the new playground is being built.

Tuesday

Multiply.

3	0	6	1	7	10	28	44	69	85
x 0	x 5	x 6	x 8	x 9	x 10	x 4	x 2	x 3	x 1

Draw and color the correct number of objects.

$2\frac{1}{3}$	$1\frac{3}{4}$	$3\frac{5}{6}$

Write adjectives on the lines to make a good story. Put periods where they are needed.

The Kingstons have a ____________ garden They grow ____________ corn, _____________ tomatoes and ____________ carrots The ___________ squirrels and ___________ bugs like the garden, too Both Mr and Mrs Kingston work very hard in their ______________ garden on the farm

Circle the correct word.

1. Jack (sit, set) the new bridle down very carefully.
2. Horses like to (lie, lay) on a soft bed of hay in a comfortable barn.
3. Please (sit, set) up straight in the saddle.
4. It is nice to be able to (lie, lay) down and take a nap when you're tired.
5. Mother (sit, set) the vase of flowers on the table.
6. Linda (sitted, sat) down slowly next to the nervous filly.

☺ ☻ ☺ **Something Special** ☺ ☻ ☺

Do an extra chore or favor for your mom or dad today, just to see them smile. It will probably make you smile, too.

Answer the questions about the portion of the dictionary page shown here.

performance - period

per·form·ance (pər-fôrməns) n. 1. The act of performing. 2. The way in which someone or something functions. 3. A presentation before an audience.

per·fume (pûr-fūm) n. 1. A liquid distilled from flowers that gives off a fragrant odor. 2. A pleasing, agreeable scent or odor.
--v. To fill with fragrance; give a pleasing odor to.

per·fum·er (pûr-fūm- ər) n. A maker or seller of perfume.

per·haps (pĕr-hăps) adv. Maybe; possibly.

per·i·dot (pĕr-ĭ-dŏt) n. A green variety of olivine used as a gem.

per·il (pĕr-əl) n. 1. A condition of imminent danger 2. Something that endangers; serious risk

pe·rim·e·ter (pə-rĭm-ĭ-tər) n. 1. a. *Math.* A closed curve bounding a plane area. b. The length of such a boundary. 2. The outer limits of an area.

1. Which of the following words would also be on this page?

perilous	punt	pillow	party
pardon	perfusion	panda	pergola

2. Which word on the page above can be used as a noun or a verb?________________

3. Which word is used in math? ____________________________

4. Which word might be the name of your birth stone? ____________________________

5. "The performance of the car was better than expected." Which definition is used in this sentence? 1 2 3

6. Use the word *perimeter* in a sentence and tell which definition you are using.

____

____

Wednesday

Subtract and check by adding.

77		84		65		71	
- 8	+ 8	- 42	+ 42	- 19	+ 19	- 26	+ 26

Use the numbers to make four equations.

4 28 7	8 40 5	6 1 6
____ x ____ = ____	____ x ____ = ____	____ x ____ = ____
____ x ____ = ____	____ x ____ = ____	____ x ____ = ____
____ ÷ ____ = ____	____ ÷ ____ = ____	____ ÷ ____ = ____
____ ÷ ____ = ____	____ ÷ ____ = ____	____ ÷ ____ = ____

Solve the story problem.

1. The town's water tower sprang a leak. It was nine minutes before the workers could get the leak stopped. If fifty gallons leaked out each minute, how much water was lost?

____

Place commas in the sentences where they belong.

1. Mr. Stevens there is a message for you on your answering machine.
2. The Jacksons raise goats pigs horses and chickens on their farm.
3. The Framptons visited Orlando Florida on their vacation.
4. I am sorry Mrs. Hollings but we have run out of size five.
5. Robins cardinals crows and ravens are all types of birds.

Place the correct punctuation at the end of each sentence. Then tell whether the sentence is **exclamatory**, **declarative** *or* **interrogative**.

________________ 1. It is fun to watch the sea gulls at the seashore

________________ 2. Look at the big claws on that crab

________________ 3. Did you bring the shovels and the buckets

________________ 4. What time will the next high tide occur

________________ 5. I think we should build a great big sand castle

Write the homonyms in the crossword puzzle.

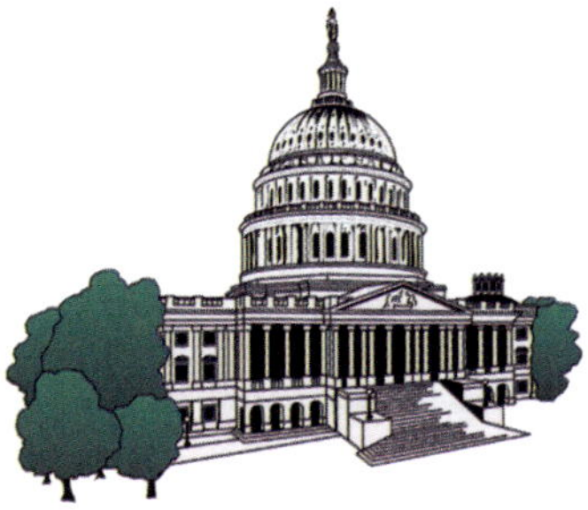

Across

3. dough
5. fare
6. blew
8. capital
9. bye
10. ad
12. heir
13. fined
14. coarse
15. be
17. creak
18. (lemon) ade
19. cent

Down

1. bawl
2. hare
3. die
4. I
5. ferry
6. bored
7. bolder
9. break
10. ant
11. flour
13. flu
16. sell
17. sealing

Divide.

$6\overline{)27}$ (4 r3)	$3\overline{)19}$	$9\overline{)50}$	$7\overline{)30}$	$5\overline{)7}$	$4\overline{)35}$
$8\overline{)20}$	$2\overline{)9}$	$10\overline{)31}$	$3\overline{)22}$	$6\overline{)14}$	$2\overline{)21}$

Look at the graph and answer the questions.

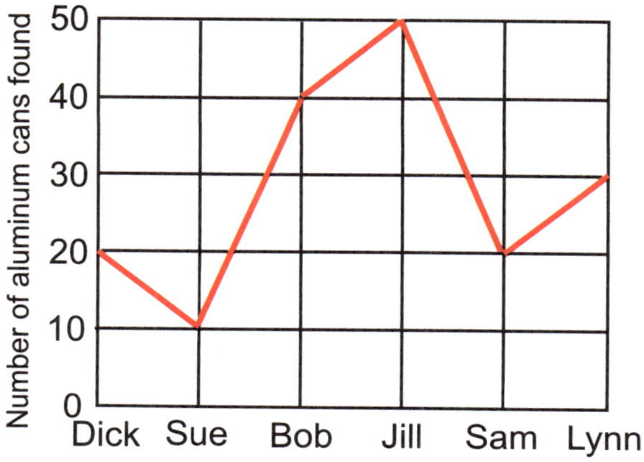

1. Who found more cans, Dick or Lynn?

   ____

2. Who found the most cans?______________
3. Which two people found the same number of cans?__________________
4. Who found the most cans, the girls or the boys? ______________________

Use the dictionary to find out which words are spelled correctly. Circle the words that are spelled correctly.

elephant - elephent

Pennsylvania - Pensylvania

squirrel -squirel

practise - practice

sentance - sentence

giraffe - girrafe

Write the plural form of each word on the line.

sheaf ______________ goose ______________ bunch ______________

fly ________________ mouse ______________ fox ________________

wolf _______________ fish _______________ rug ________________

guppy ______________ deer _______________

Try This!
Get two small balls and see if you can learn to juggle them with one hand.

Starting with the word you are given, change one letter each time to make a new word.

meat

1. to hit something a lot — b e a t
2. a small, round ball used in a necklace or bracelet ____ ____ ____ ____
3. to form a curve with force or pressure ____ ____ ____ ____
4. to let someone borrow, especially money ____ ____ ____ ____
5. ground; opposite of sea ____ ____ ____ ____
6. road or small street ____ ____ ____ ____
7. the shaggy hair on a male lion ____ ____ ____ ____
8. opposite of female ____ ____ ____ ____
9. 5,280 feet ____ ____ ____ ____
10. pleasant; far from extreme ____ ____ ____ ____
11. the stuff that grows on old bread ____ ____ ____ ____
12. a state of feeling, such as happy or sad ____ ____ ____ ____
13. what shines at night ____ ____ ____ ____
14. a groan, often from pain ____ ____ ____ ____
15. not nice; rude or ugly in behavior ____ ____ ____ ____
16. chicken, beef, or fish ____ ____ ____ ____

Friday

Tell whether the number is odd or even.

461 ________	8 ________	99 ________	6392 ________
32 ________	63 ________	474 ________	740 ________
7864 ________	935 ________	9761 ________	1 ________

Solve the story problems.

1. Valerie saw 6 birds, 4 butterflies, 27 ants, 5 crickets and 2 deer in the woods near her house. How many insects did she see?

____

2. Mr. Andersen made $40 for working 8 hours last Thursday. How much did he make an hour?

____

3. If Janet earns $162 a week, how much money does she earn in four weeks?

____

4. Mr. and Mrs. McCollum went on a 497 mile trip. They went 235 miles on the first day. How many more miles do they need to travel on the second day?

____

Put quotation marks where they belong.

Can you come over to my house? asked Ned. I would like to show you my new fish.

I don't know, answered Peter. I will have to ask my mom. Can you wait a minute?

Yes, I'll wait, said Ned. Hurry up and ask her. I want to show the fish to you before lunch.

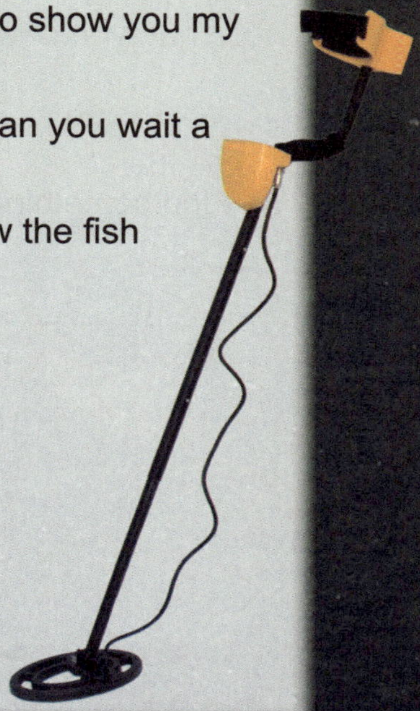

Underline each subject once and each verb twice.

1. My dad and I look for treasure together on weekends.
2. We use a metal detector, and we take a shovel with us.
3. Sometimes we find coins or locate old nails.
4. One Saturday I found a bracelet, and my dad found a knife.
5. Maybe one day we will find a really important treasure.

Sheep Shearing

from *McGuffey's Second Eclectic Reader*

Sheep are washed and sheared some time in the month of June. This should be done quite early in the month, before the hot days begin.

It is fun for the people watching, but not much fun for the sheep. It is best for the sheep to have the wool taken off. Otherwise, they would be too hot in the summertime.

When the time comes for washing the sheep, they are driven to a pond or a little river. Then they are thrown into the water, one at a time. The men who are in the water catch them, and squeeze the wet wool with their hands to get the dirt out of it.

When the wool is thoroughly dried, the sheep are taken to the shearer. He cuts off the wool with a large pair of shears. It is then dyed, spun, and woven into cloth.

In a short time, before the cold winter comes, new wool grows out on the sheep. By spring time there is so much that it must be cut off again.

Answer the questions about what you read.

1. Why do sheep need to be sheared? ____

   ____

2. Why are the sheep thrown into a pond?

   to cool off   to be washed   to have fun swimming

3. Write a synonym for the word *shears*. ____

4. What type of writing is this selection?

   a story   information   a poem   an advertisement

5. Find something in your house that is made with wool. What color is it? __________

Add.

$2.87	106	428	$3.04	195	465	$1.79
+ 0.96	+ 354	+ 48	+ 2.86	+ 46	+ 535	+ 3.77

Use the numbers to make four math facts.

9 14 5

____ + ____ = ____
____ + ____ = ____
____ - ____ = ____
____ - ____ = ____

3 11 8

____ + ____ = ____
____ + ____ = ____
____ - ____ = ____
____ - ____ = ____

8 15 7

____ + ____ = ____
____ + ____ = ____
____ - ____ = ____
____ - ____ = ____

Fill in the temperatures.

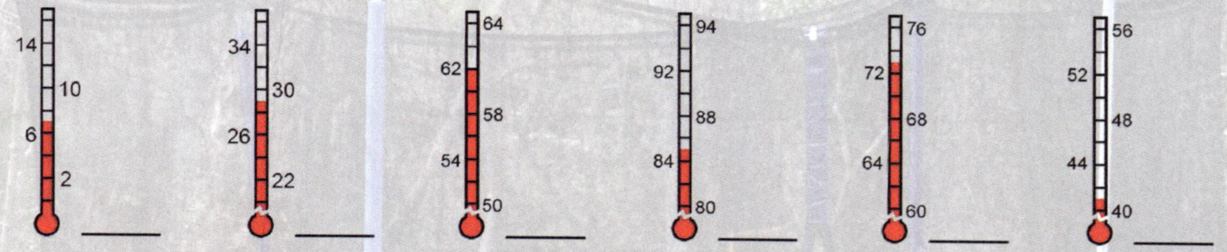

____ ____ ____ ____ ____ ____

Put a ✓ over the underlined word if it is a noun. Put an **X** *over the underlined word if it is not a noun.*

<u>Dave</u> and Holly have a trampoline <u>in</u> their <u>backyard</u>. They love to <u>jump</u> on it <u>and</u> do tricks. Dave <u>usually</u> practices a front <u>flip</u> which is his favorite <u>trick</u>. Holly, who takes <u>gymnastics</u>, often <u>works</u> on a jump called a Russian <u>or</u> toe touch.

On most <u>days</u> Dave <u>and</u> Holly have <u>friends</u> who come and jump <u>with</u> them. But all the <u>friends</u> are very <u>careful</u> to obey the safety <u>rules</u> so that they <u>can</u> all have fun.

Put an X on the letters that should be capitalized and write the capital over them.

1. valentine's day comes on february 14th.
2. mr. smithers really enjoys collecting stamps from south america.
3. do you know if the meeting will be on wednesday or thursday?
4. our new home is at 275 mountain view parkway in lacey spring, virginia.

Make a new word and write it on the line. There may be more than one word that can be made from the letters. Any good word is a fine answer.

Example: get + a = gate goat - o = tag

1. super - s = ______________________________

2. bus + s = ______________________________

3. dairy - y = ______________________________

4. fat + s = ______________________________

5. heart - h = ______________________________

6. grin + w = ______________________________

7. page - e = ______________________________

8. plead + e = ______________________________

9. weep - e = ______________________________

10. barrel - r = ______________________________

Tuesday

Multiply.

2 x 7 = ______ 0 x 0 = ______ 4 x 4 = ______ 7 x 1 = ______

8 x 8 = ______ 1 x 9 = ______ 5 x 10 = ______ 2 x 6 = ______

3 x 2 = ______ 6 x 7 = ______ 9 x 5 = ______ 10 x 3 = ______

Write the correct fraction.

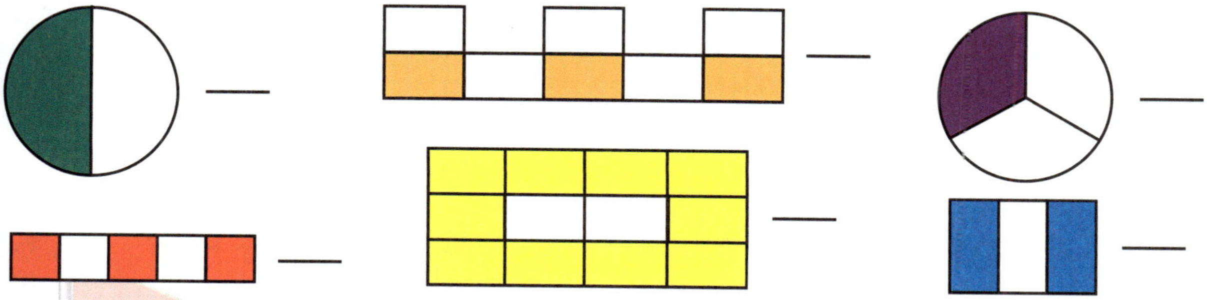

Put periods in the story where they belong.

Mr B L Harrison is my neighbor Mr Harrison raises Dalmatians His good friend, Dr Cox, comes over at least once a week to check on Mr Harrison's dogs Both men love dogs I am glad to have such an interesting neighbor right here on Hanover St

Remember, adjectives are words that describe something. Underline the adjectives and draw an arrow to the word it describes.

1. Dr. Abrams, our local doctor, loves to play golf at the new golf course.
2. The new course has fresh green grass and bright flags.
3. Many of the men like to drive the shiny new golf carts.
4. The golf shop at the course sells many kinds of clubs and special clothes.

☺ ***Just For Fun*** ☺

Draw some faces or animals on balloons. Blow them up and watch what happens to your drawings.

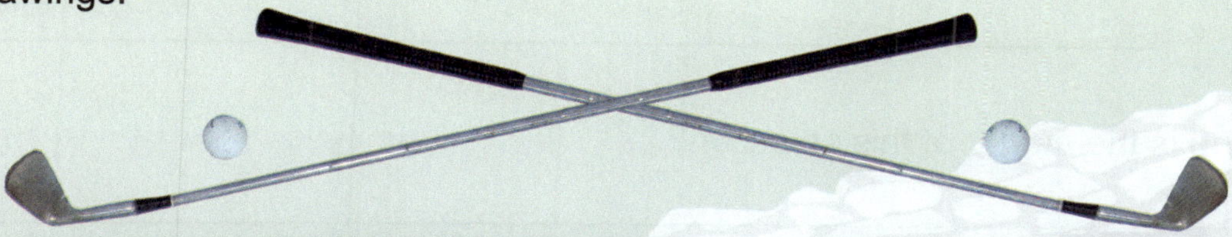

It Isn't Costly
by Edgar A. Guest

Does the grouch get richer quicker than the friendly sort of man?
Can the grumbler labor better than the cheerful fellow can?
Is the mean and churlish neighbor any cleverer than the one
Who shouts a glad "good morning," and then smiling passes on?
Just stop and think about it. Have you ever known or seen
A mean man who succeeded, just because he was so mean?

When you find a grouch with honors and with money in his pouch,
You can bet he didn't win them just because he was a grouch.
Oh, you'll not be any poorer if you smile along your way,
And your lot will not be harder for the kindly things you say.
Don't imagine you are wasting time for others that you spend:
You can rise to wealth and glory and still pause to be a friend.

Answer the questions about what you read.

1. What type of writing is this? poem story chapter

2. In one sentence write the main idea of this selection.

____

3. List three things that will not change in life just because you are grouchy.

   a. ____

   b. ____

   c. ____

4. Who is the author of this selection?

____

Wednesday

Subtract.

900	615	881	623	965	512	751	818
- 244	- 426	- 294	- 86	- 439	- 178	- 347	- 99

Put **<** *or* **>** *in the circle.*

10 - 5 ◯ 42 ÷ 7	17 - 8 ◯ 15 - 8	36 ÷ 6 ◯ 72 ÷ 8	48 ÷ 6 ◯ 12 - 6
13 - 6 ◯ 72 ÷ 9	15 - 9 ◯ 14 - 9	49 ÷ 7 ◯ 25 ÷ 5	45 ÷ 9 ◯ 13 - 5
15 - 6 ◯ 40 ÷ 8	12 - 7 ◯ 15 - 7	45 ÷ 5 ◯ 35 ÷ 5	81 ÷ 9 ◯ 14 - 8

What comes next?

2, 4, ______, ______, ______, ______, ______, ______, ______

4, 8, ______, ______, ______, ______, ______, ______, ______

6, 12, ______, ______, ______, ______, ______, ______, ______

Circle the correct word.

1. Brendan received a (knew, new) pair of stilts last week.
2. (Dew, Do) you know if he (asked, axed) for help with them?
3. Did anyone (sea, see) if he fell down a lot or (knot, not)?
4. Now Brendan can walk back and (forth, fourth) easily on his stilts.
5. Little Joe wants (to, too, two) try the stilts (himself, hisself).

Place commas where they belong in the paragraph.

On June 16 2005 we moved from Greenville North Carolina to Kewanee Illinois. We were in our new house and unpacked by June 21 2005. I liked our new home. It had three bedrooms two bathrooms a living room a dining room and a kitchen. My brother Nathan liked the backyard the best. It had a few good climbing trees a creek and lots of room for running around.

Finish labeling the graph and filling it in using the information you are given. Then answer the questions from your graph.

The neighborhood kids decided to set up an obstacle course and have a contest to see who could do it the fastest. They practiced all week and held the contest on Saturday. Their times were: Sandra - 6 min.; Benjamin - 4 min.; Nathan - 5 min.; Zena - 7 min.; Steve - 3 min.; Renee - 5 min.

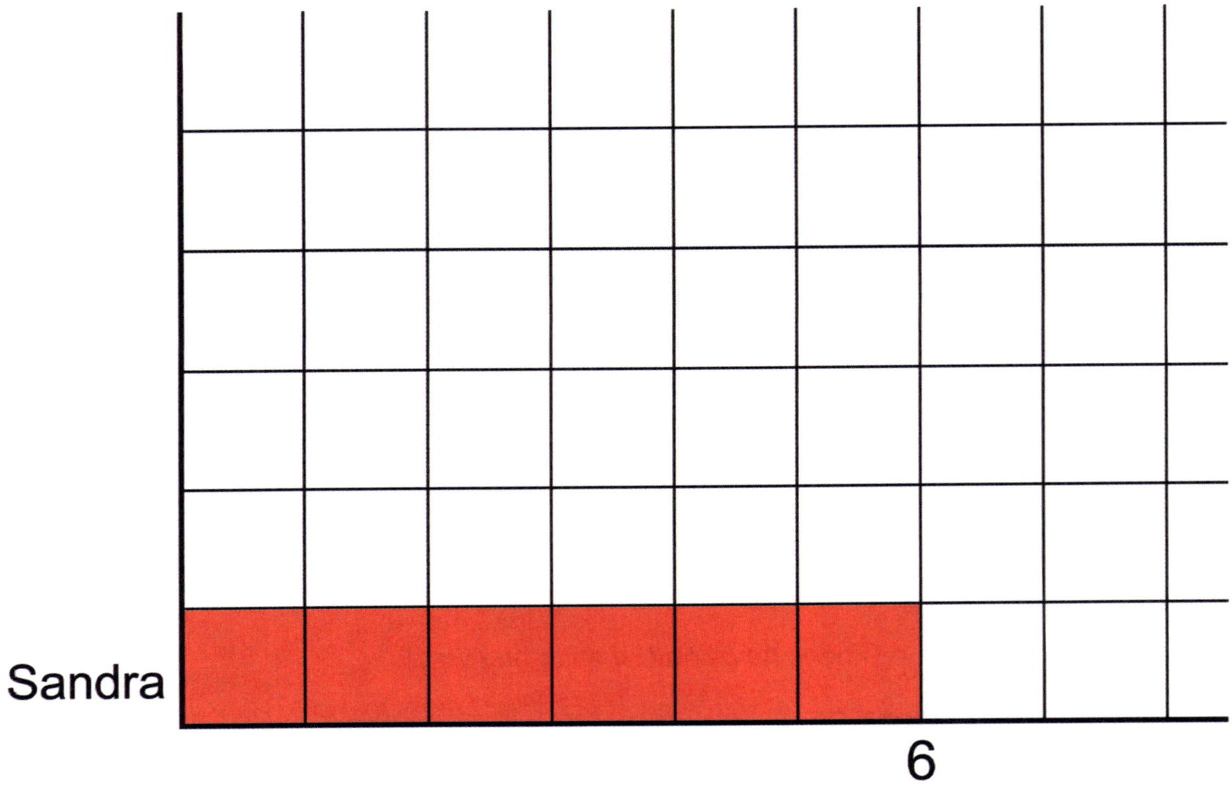

1. Who finished the obstacle course the fastest? ____________________

2. Which two took the same amount of time? ____________________

3. How many minutes difference is there between the fastest and slowest times?

   ____

4. If the boys raced the girls as teams, which team do you think would win? Why?

   ____

Thursday

Divide.

81 ÷ 9 = ______ 8 ÷ 2 = ______ 27 ÷ 3 = ______ 24 ÷ 4 = ______

24 ÷ 6 = ______ 0 ÷ 1 = ______ 36 ÷ 9 = ______ 56 ÷ 7 = ______

15 ÷ 3 = ______ 7 ÷ 1 = ______ 42 ÷ 7 = ______ 24 ÷ 8 = ______

Add.

83	239	99	86	563	332	281	43
566	48	14	378	193	61	526	54
+ 12	+ 37	+ 452	+ 117	+ 56	+ 449	+ 175	+ 67

Choose three of the incomplete sentences below and rewrite them to make complete sentences.

a gray goose running away and yelling the bright, red car

a red, white and blue flag giggling and laughing

____

____

____

____

____

Write the plural form of each word on the line.

match ______________ shelf ______________ child ______________

ox ______________ six ______________ chair ______________

life ______________ man ______________ hand ______________

bug ______________ wolf ______________ dress ______________

Hint Hunter

The Stokes children earned money doing extra chores during the week. Little Danny earned enough money to buy a small candy bar. Dianne earned the most and hoped she could buy a new pair of shoes. Duran wanted to use his money to get a hamburger and fries with his dad. Debbie wanted to buy a new necklace but does not have enough money. She put her money in her wallet and saved it. How much did each child earn?

Danny 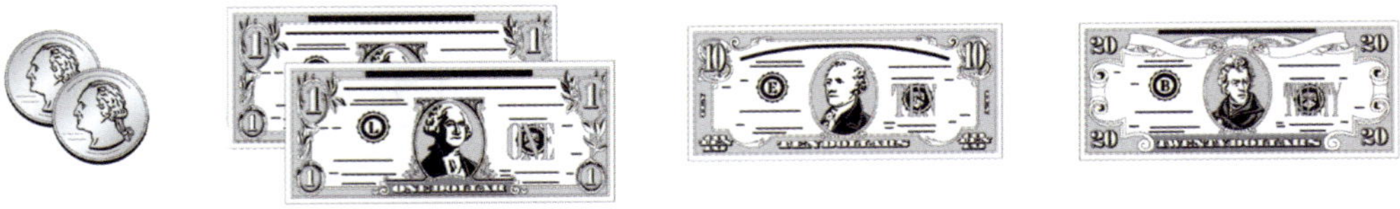

Debbie 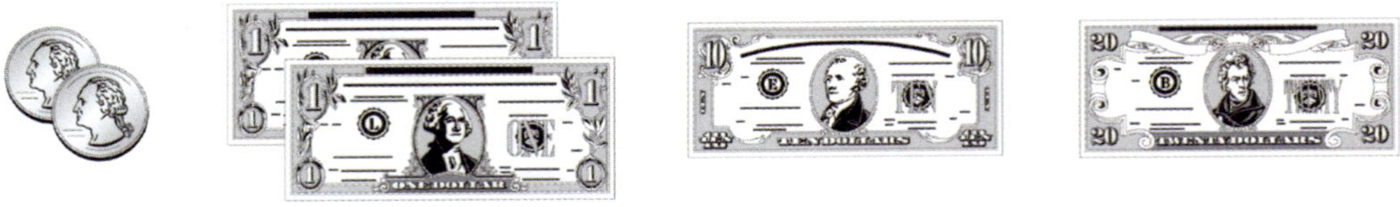

Dianne 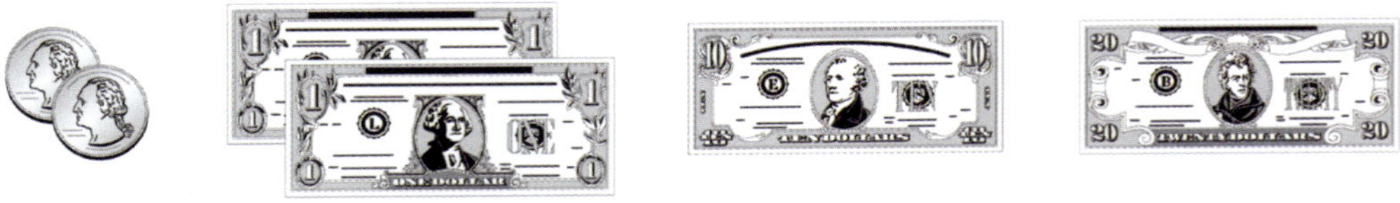

Duran 

Friday

Solve these story problems.

1. Mrs. Parks has 28 apples, 6 of which are green. She divided them evenly among 4 of her neighbors. How many did she give each neighbor?

____

2. Mark and Melvin are brothers. They are saving for a puppy. So far they have each saved $4.75. The puppy costs $20. How much more do they need to save?

____

3. The 4th grade class held a car wash to raise money to go on a special field trip. Each child needed to earn $36. If each child is paid $4 per car, how many cars does each child need to wash?

____

In what place is the zero?

40 ____________	90,835 ____________	10 ____________
607 ____________	205,624 ____________	409 ____________
10,357 ____________	106 ____________	5,032 ____________
890 ____________	706,318 ____________	50,927 ____________

*Write synonyms for the **bold** words to make a good sentence.*

yard 1. David, it is your turn to mow the ____________.

boat 2. That large ____________ is an aircraft carrier.

violet 3. ____________ is my favorite color.

quick 4. A cheetah can run very ____________.

carpet 5. Denise, please do not let your muddy shoes get on the new ________.

Circle the verbs.

1. An Ultra-Soaker-Supreme is a great water gun.
2. My friends and I have big water fights on hot afternoons.
3. We run and hide and surprise each other.
4. The cold water feels really good when I am hot and sweaty.

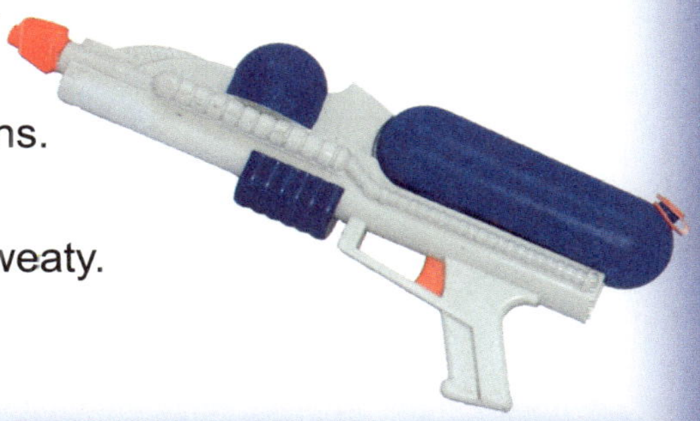

from *The Daddy Series for Little Folks*
by Howard Garis

Hal and Mab Blake lived with Daddy and Mother in a nice house in a small city. Uncle Pennywait and Aunt Lollipop lived with them. These were not their real names. Uncle Pennywait was called that because he so often said to Hal and Mab, "Wait a minute, and I'll give you a penny!" Aunt Lollipop was more often called Aunt Lolly. The reason she had such a queer name was because she was always telling the children to buy lollipops with the money Uncle Pennywait gave them. Lollipops, the children's aunt thought, were the best kind of candy for them. Perhaps she was right. Then there was Roly-Poly, the funny little poodle dog. Once when Daddy took Hal and Mab skating, Roly slid under the ice and was lost for a long, long time.

Hal and Mab just loved to go places with Daddy. They learned about the birds, trees and flowers. They had gone to the circus with him and sailing. They had hunted birds with a camera and taken pictures of them. They had many adventures each time they went out, and they learned many things.

Answer the questions about the story.

1. Why was Uncle Pennywait given his name? ______________________________

____

2. Why was Aunt Lolly given her name? ______________________________

____

3. Roly-Poly is the name of the Blake's __________.

dog insect brother sister

4. Write two sentences about something you have learned from your dad. ________

____

____

____

____

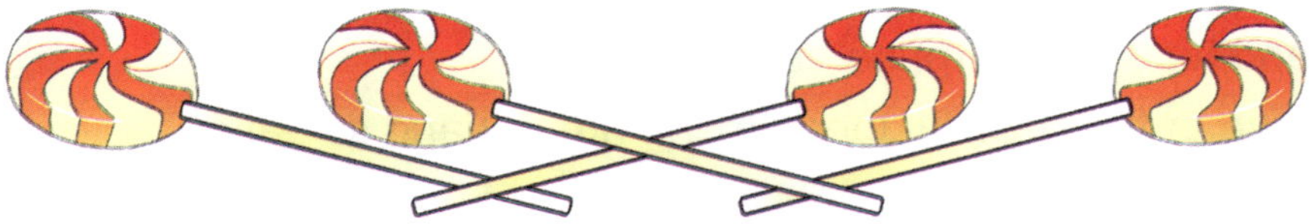

Add.

62	21	65	87	16	24	74	51	94	80
+ 57	+ 85	+ 8	+ 44	+ 53	+ 9	+ 19	+ 37	+ 10	+ 35

Subtract to find how much change should be made. Draw coins to show the change.

Nancy bought some yarn for $1.47. She paid $2.00.	Larry bought an airplane kit for $5.75. He paid $6.00.
Greg bought a model ship for $4.14. He paid $4.25.	Mary bought some fabric for $2.41. She paid $2.50.

Write a noun on each line to make an interesting story.
Then circle the letters that should be capitalized.

i like to skate in my rollerblades on the _____________. sometimes _____________ and _____________ come over and we all skate together. we like to race each other and play _______________. the cracks and the _____________ in the driveway can be a problem, though.

Write the contraction on the line.

should have ______________________ will not ________________________

cannot __________________________ let us __________________________

they have _______________________ who is __________________________

Circle the operation(s) you need to do to solve the problem. Then solve the problem.

1. The Sinclairs decided to serve a buffet of fresh fruit at a party on Saturday. They bought 3 mega-melons at $7.75 each, strawberries for $7.25, apples for $4.95, pears for $6.15, and figs for $8.10. How much did they spend on fruit?

Step 1: + - x ÷

Step 2: + - x ÷

Answer:

2. Mrs. Thomas bought 4 pounds of apples for $2.75 per pound. How much did she pay for apples?

Step 1: + - x ÷

Answer:

3. Blueberries are $3 a pint. How many pints can be bought for $12?

Step 1: + - x ÷

Answer:

4. Regular watermelons are $4.95 each. Mega-melons are $7.75 each. How much less is a regular watermelon than a mega-melon?

Step 1: + - x ÷

Answer:

☆5. Mrs. Gantry bought 5 pounds of apples for $2.75 per pound and 3 pounds of pears for $4.15 per pound. How much change did she get from two twenty dollar bills?

Step 1: + - x ÷

Step 2: + - x ÷

Step 3: + - x ÷

Step 4: + - x ÷

Answer:

Multiply.

5	2	8	9	10	30	51	79	97	4
x 5	x 4	x 0	x 6	x 7	x 6	x 3	x 2	x 8	x 10

Color the correct amount of each shape.

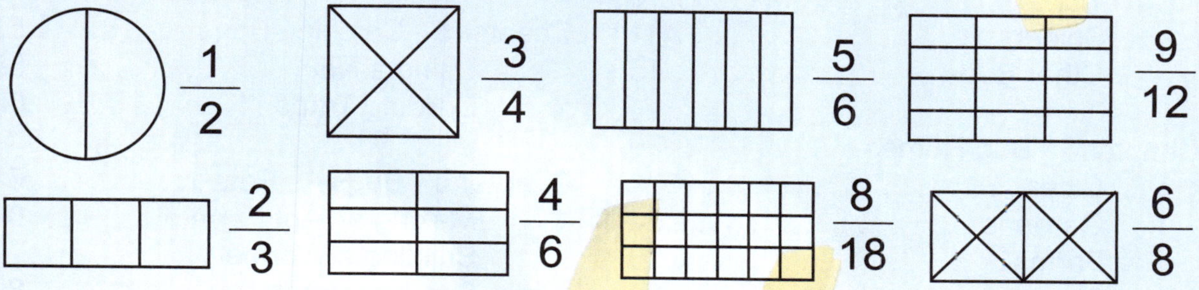

Solve this story problem.

1. Andy feeds twenty-seven cows, five sheep and fourteen goats each morning. How many animals does he feed each morning?

____

Put periods in the sentences where they belong.

1. I live at 421 Redwood Cir in Thompson, Mass
2. Denise has never met Mrs Jennifer G Hartman
3. Sammy has grown to be 4 ft and 3 in tall
4. Holly visits Mrs Teal on Wed afternoons
5. Dr S McDuff is my favorite dentist

Circle the adjectives in the story.

Tanner's yellow foam airplane is a nice airplane. The long wings are adjustable and so are the tail fins. Tanner can make his plane fly in a straight line by adjusting the wings and tail a certain way. If he moves the wings another way, he can make his plane fly in a loop.

Sometimes Tanner puts a small weight on either the nose or the tail of the airplane. The small weight causes the airplane to fly differently. Tanner really enjoys experimenting with his yellow plane.

Answer the questions about the table of contents.

Contents

Chapter 1 - Bugs Are Everywhere! . . . 1

Chapter 2 - Not All Bugs Are Insects . 5
- Insect Characteristics 6
- Ticks 8
- Spiders 11
- Other Bugs 15

Chapter 3 - Bug Homes 20
- Cities 21
- Gardens 24
- Farms 29
- Forests 31
- Waterways 34
- Mountains 37
- Deserts 39

Chapter 4 - Bug Eating Habits. 42
- Plant Eaters 43
- Animal Eaters 46
- Other Odd Foods 49

Chapter 5 - Catching Bugs 57
- Using a Net 58
- Building Traps 60

Chapter 6 - Bugs As Pets 63
- Making an Ant Farm 64
- Building a Wormery 71
- Bee Keeping 80

Glossary 95

1. Which chapter has the most sections? _______ The fewest? ______

2. To what page would you turn to read about bugs that live in creeks? ______

3. If you wanted to start a bee hive in your yard for fresh honey, what section should you read? ____

   On what page does this section begin? ______

4. If your family were going camping in the mountains and you wanted to see what kinds of bugs might be around your campsite, what section would you read?

   ____

   On what page does this section begin? ______

5. What is a "Glossary"?
   a. a list of other good books to read
   b. a list of words found in the book and their definitions
   c. a large collection of pictures

Subtract.

\$52.36	4,311	6,488	\$39.81	2,442	6,013
- 4.75	- 547	- 620	- 3.99	- 776	- 555

Use the numbers to make four math facts.

8 72 9	3 12 4	9 36 4
____ x ____ = ____	____ x ____ = ____	____ x ____ = ____
____ x ____ = ____	____ x ____ = ____	____ x ____ = ____
____ ÷ ____ = ____	____ ÷ ____ = ____	____ ÷ ____ = ____
____ ÷ ____ = ____	____ ÷ ____ = ____	____ ÷ ____ = ____

Tell whether the sentence is **declarative, interrogative** *or* **exclamatory**.

____________ 1. It was fun to build a tree swing with Dad.

____________ 2. Don't run into the tree!

____________ 3. Would you like a turn on the swing?

____________ 4. I like to try to climb the rope.

____________ 5. Do you have a tall tree in your yard?

Put commas where they belong.

1. No you may not sleep outside in this weather.
2. Kevin you can play basketball very well.
3. Sarah I am pleased with the way you have practiced the piano.
4. Laura Peter Walter and Julia went on the hike last Saturday.
5. My mother was born August 14 1972 and my father was born the year before that.

??? What is the capital of your state? ______________________________

Look at the items in each row. Tell why the other items belong together and add another item to the group.

Example: banana apple pear grapes
Why? *The items are all fruits. orange*

1. pebble boulder stone

   Why? ______________________________

2. plate cup spoon

   Why? ______________________________

3. robin cardinal wren

   Why? ______________________________

4. skirt shirt blouse tie

   Why? ______________________________

5. Florida California Minnesota

   Why? ______________________________

6. skates wagon bike

   Why? ______________________________

7. Barry Benjamin Bryan

   Why? ______________________________

8. ice cream cottage cheese yogurt

   Why? ______________________________

9. bunk twin double

   Why? ______________________________

10. Stephanie Sarah Sylvia

    Why? ______________________________

Thursday

Divide.

3 ÷ 1 = _____ 48 ÷ 6 = _____ 5 ÷ 1 = _____ 25 ÷ 5 = _____

0 ÷ 9 = _____ 35 ÷ 5 = _____ 4 ÷ 2 = _____ 15 ÷ 3 = _____

6 ÷ 3 = _____ 14 ÷ 7 = _____ 6 ÷ 1 = _____ 63 ÷ 9 = _____

Decide whether you should use inches, feet, or yards to measure these things.

the length of your driveway __________ the width of this page __________

how tall you are __________ the length of your shoe __________

the width of the living room __________ the height of the table __________

Number the words in each column in alphabetical order.

_____ pansy	_____ sheets	_____ stand	_____ beans
_____ petal	_____ pillows	_____ skip	_____ broccoli
_____ purple	_____ pink	_____ saunter	_____ beets
_____ petunia	_____ pajamas	_____ sit	_____ Brussels sprouts

Write the plural form of each word on the line.

lunch _______________ loaf _______________ foot _______________

ax _______________ bag _______________ puppy _______________

Underline each subject once and each verb twice.

1. Nine boys practiced Hi-Li scoop ball in the empty lot in the neighborhood.
2. They caught and threw the ball with the scoops very well.
3. Tomorrow the boys will divide into teams and play a regular game.

Answer the questions.

1. A train going west passes by the station every two hours. If the most recent westbound train went by at 11:30 a. m., when should the station master expect the next westbound train?

2. The Goldline Express travels from Empire City to Capital Landing in fourteen hours without stopping. If the train leaves Empire City at 7:00 a. m., when will it arrive in Capital Landing?

3. The mail train stops at Tinytown at 8:12 a. m. every morning. It stops in Berryburg exactly thirty-five minutes later. Twenty minutes after that it stops in Hartsville. What time does the train stop in Hartsville each day?

4. Mr. Clarendon takes a forty-five minute train ride home from work each day. If he arrives at 6:15 p. m., what time did his ride begin?

5. Mr. and Mrs. Wiggins are going out west to see the Grand Canyon. The train trip is supposed to take twenty-three hours. If they leave on Wednesday at 6:00 p. m., what day and time will they arrive?

6. The train trip from Gettysburg to Remington was supposed to take three hours, but it was delayed by twenty-three minutes. If the train was supposed to arrive at 8:45 p. m., what time did it actually pull into the station?

Fill in the missing numbers.

5 + _____ = 10	9 x _____ = 63	7 + _____ = 16	8 x _____ = 40
6 + _____ = 12	7 x _____ = 56	6 + _____ = 15	6 x _____ = 30
9 + _____ = 16	5 x _____ = 40	7 + _____ = 13	6 x _____ = 42

Solve these story problems.

1. If it is 437 miles from Greenville, SC, to Pensacola, FL, how many miles is it for a round trip?

____

2. Bill is saving money to buy a $27 skateboard. So far he has $18. How much more does he need?

____

3. How many days are in 3 years?

____

4. Mr. Greene drove 117 miles on a trip. Then he stopped for lunch and paid $4.37. After lunch he drove 193 more miles. How far did he drive in all?

____

Put quotation marks where they belong.

What would you like to play today? asked Elizabeth.

I don't know, answered Grace. We played hide and seek yesterday and house the day before that. What do you think we should do?

Why don't we draw with the sidewalk chalk? suggested Elizabeth.

Add the missing punctuation and tell whether the sentence is a **declarative** *or* **interrogative** *sentence.*

_____________ 1. Helen and Maggie like to toss the fuzzy ball

_____________ 2. They catch the ball with their velcro catchers

_____________ 3. Who catches the ball the most, Helen or Maggie

_____________ 4. Does this sound like fun to you

_____________ 5. The girls like to think of strange ways to catch the ball

The White Giant
from *The Tale of Jolly Robin*

Jolly Robin was frightened. He saw a strange man. It was not Farmer Green or the hired man. This was a giant! He had big, black eyes and a great lump of a nose. The nose stuck out strangely from his face. He was dressed in all white and had an old, black hat. In one hand he held a stick. Jolly Robin was just about to go back to the farmhouse when he saw somebody come running toward the orchard. "Here's Johnnie Green!"

Jolly saw Johnnie Green stop and make an armful of snowballs. Then he went straight to the man in white. Johnnie began to shout, but the man in white did not move. Johnnie Green threw a snowball at the man. The snowball knocked off the man's hat. Jolly Robin was more surprised than ever because the man did not even turn his head!

"That's strange," said Jolly Robin to himself. "He must be asleep, but I should think he would wake up."

Answer the questions about the story.

1. What was the white giant? ______________________________

2. List three clues that told you who the white giant was.

____

____

____

3. What animal is Jolly Robin? ______________________________

4. Johnnie Green is probably a(n) __________. man boy animal

How do you know? ______________________________

____

Monday

Add.

156	395	268	336	427	464	376
+ 477	+ 434	+ 189	+ 549	+ 285	+ 148	+ 597

Use each set of numbers to make four math facts.

8 17 9	5 13 8	6 13 7
____ + ____ = ____	____ + ____ = ____	____ + ____ = ____
____ + ____ = ____	____ + ____ = ____	____ + ____ = ____
____ - ____ = ____	____ - ____ = ____	____ - ____ = ____
____ - ____ = ____	____ - ____ = ____	____ - ____ = ____

What comes next?

3, 6, ______, ______, ______, ______, ______, ______, ______

5, 10, ______, ______, ______, ______, ______, ______, ______

7, 14, ______, ______, ______, ______, ______, ______, ______

Underline the words that need a capital letter.

1. last june grandpa and grandma lesley, who live in vermont, came to visit us.
2. the parade will start at the mall, travel down main street, and end at redlane park.
3. cindy and kathy are bob's and david's cousins.
4. “the star-spangled banner” is our national anthem.
5. what month comes before october?

Circle all the nouns in these sentences.

1. Ben loves to ride his scooter up and down the driveway and sidewalk.
2. The handles are covered in soft foam.
3. The back wheel has a great brake.
4. Ben has had the scooter for three years.
5. His friends, Jerry and Mike, also have scooters and the boys like to have races.

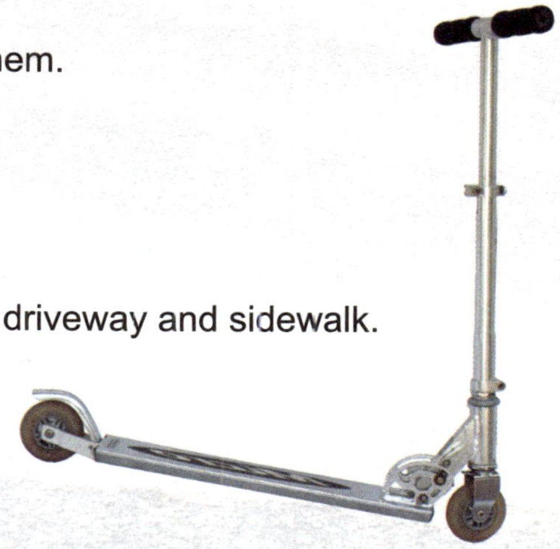

Answer the questions about the map.

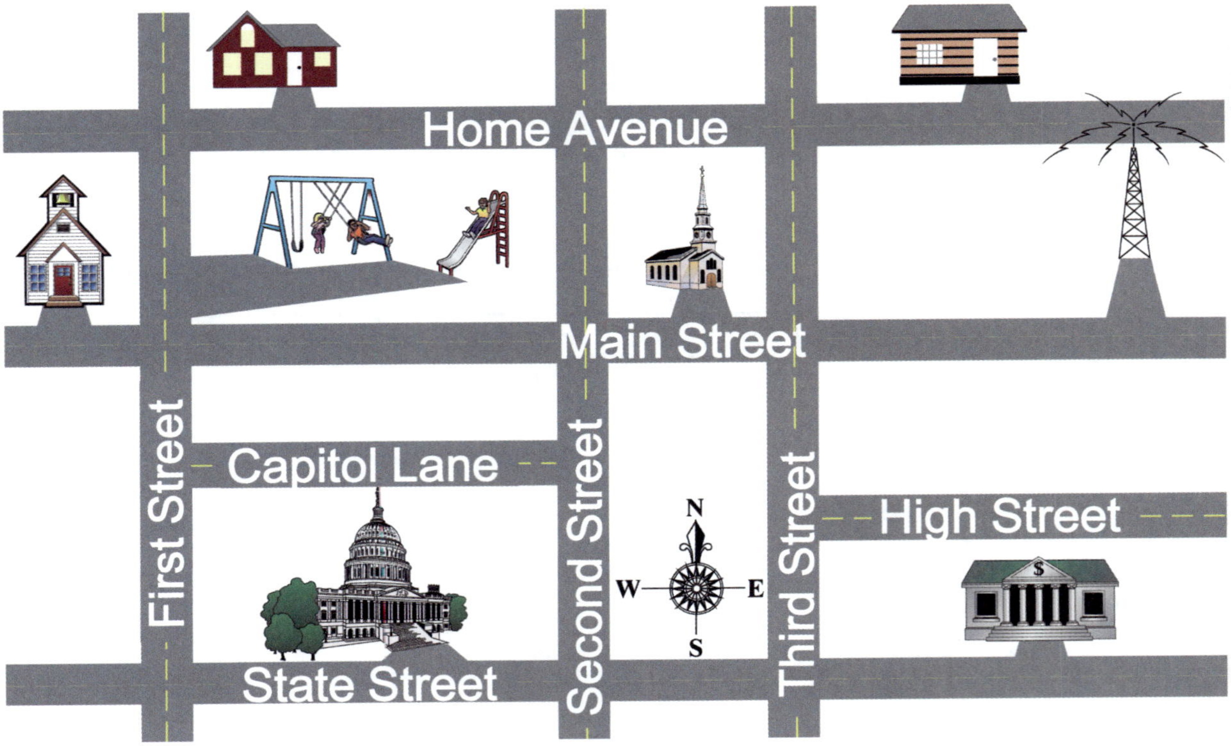

1. When driving from the bank to the capitol, which streets would you cross?

____

2. The Jones family lives at the west end of Home Avenue. Each day Mr. Jones drives to his job at the radio tower by the shortest route. Does he drive on High Street?

____

3. Explain how to get from the school to the capitol building.

____

____

4. Explain how to drive from the radio tower to the playground.

____

____

Multiply.

3 x 1 = _____ 1 x 10 = _____ 5 x 3 = _____ 7 x 5 = _____

9 x 0 = _____ 6 x 2 = _____ 4 x 6 = _____ 3 x 5 = _____

10 x 8 = _____ 8 x 1 = _____ 2 x 9 = _____ 0 x 4 = _____

Write a mixed number to show how much has been shaded.

 _____

 _____

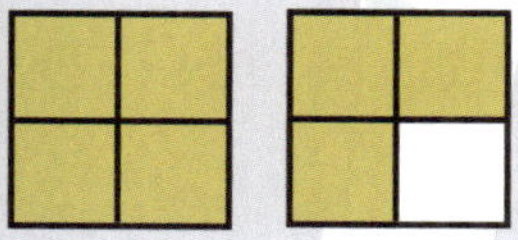 _____

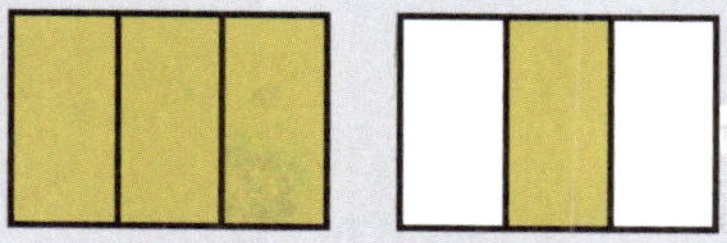 _____

Put periods where they belong.

Mr and Mrs Timmons own the farm at the end of Rt 99 They raise horses Mr Timmons is especially proud of his Tennessee Walkers These horses are very beautiful and quite comfortable to ride Mrs Timmons raises miniature ponies as a hobby Some people come and buy them and keep them in their houses as pets I like to go to their farm and pet all the horses

Write an adjective on the line to make a good sentence.

1. The ______________________ flowers smelled very sweet.
2. The grasshopper quickly hopped into the _____________ weeds.
3. The __________________ lantern shone brightly.
4. _____________ children were snuggled in their sleeping bags in the tent.
5. I like camping in the __________________ woods.

??? Do you know how tall you are? Have someone measure you to the nearest inch.

I am ____ feet and ____ inches tall.

Find the names of twenty-four states in the puzzle. Be very careful. Some state names have been spelled incorrectly to try to trick you. Only circle the name of each state when it is spelled correctly.

R	V	S	X	W	N	P	E	N	N	E	B	R	A	S	C	A	R
H	O	O	E	T	I	N	E	T	N	E	N	T	O	H	I	O	N
O	K	U	M	U	E	S	V	N	E	E	B	E	E	D	P	R	O
D	L	T	W	O	N	N	C	E	N	X	W	R	V	X	E	A	R
E	A	H	E	N	N	O	N	O	R	S	A	Y	A	E	A	G	T
I	H	C	N	E	O	T	R	E	N	M	Y	S	O	S	D	O	H
S	O	A	W	W	R	R	A	T	S	S	O	L	U	R	K	N	D
L	M	R	Y	M	E	W	T	N	H	S	I	N	V	T	K	A	A
A	A	O	O	E	G	N	N	H	A	C	E	N	T	A	E	W	K
N	Y	L	M	X	O	N	E	V	A	D	A	E	N	W	N	H	O
D	U	I	I	I	N	P	N	E	W	J	E	R	S	E	Y	I	T
H	T	N	N	C	S	O	U	T	H	D	A	K	O	T	A	E	A
S	A	A	G	O	W	Y	O	M	M	I	N	G	I	L	A	N	D
A	H	R	N	E	W	H	A	M	P	S	H	I	R	E	I	W	V
W	A	S	H	I	N	G	T	O	N	P	E	N	S	Y	L	N	A
W	E	S	T	V	I	R	G	I	N	I	A	O	R	G	O	N	A

Montana
Nebraska
Nevada
New Hampshire
New Jersey
New Mexico
New York
North Carolina
North Dakota
Ohio
Oklahoma
Oregon
Pennsylvania
Rhode Island
South Carolina
South Dakota
Tennessee
Texas
Utah
Vermont
Washington
West Virginia
Wisconsin
Wyoming

Wednesday

Subtract and check by adding.

90		59		56		93	
- 33	+ 33	- 11	+ 11	- 7	+ 7	- 20	+ 20

Put **<** *or* **>** *in the circle.*

8 + 1 ◯ 2 + 2	13 - 5 ◯ 11 - 4	13 - 6 ◯ 3 + 1	13 - 8 ◯ 4 + 5
8 + 6 ◯ 7 + 9	10 - 5 ◯ 12 - 9	11 - 8 ◯ 1 + 1	14 - 7 ◯ 6 + 3
5 + 6 ◯ 8 + 2	17 - 9 ◯ 11- 2	17 - 8 ◯ 3 + 9	10 - 6 ◯ 1 + 2

Write **our, your,** *or* **their** *on the lines.*

1. ________ house is going to be painted this summer before we move.
2. "Please raise ________ hand before speaking," said the teacher.
3. The children quickly licked ________ ice cream cones to keep them from dripping.
4. Please clean up ________ own room, George.
5. Many men wash and wax ________ cars on Saturday.

Circle the adjectives in the sentences.

1. The old basketball swished through the high net.
2. Four small boys played on the wide driveway in the early sunshine.
3. In the late afternoon, the older boys played an active game of basketball.
4. Kevin actually prefers to practice his free throws and other shots.
5. The boys like it the best when dad has time to play with them.

Circle the correct word.

1. Mother, (may, can) I go over to James' house for the afternoon?
2. Did you know that Penny (may, can) tie her shoe all by herself?
3. For lunch I have (a, an) sandwich and (a, an) apple.
4. Do you have (a, an) pair of scissors that I could borrow?
5. The (children's, childrens') game was finished.
6. The (van's, vans) motor is making a strange sound.

Fill in each blank with the best word from the bottom of the page.

George Washington Carver grew up to be a ________________ who tried to understand every plant and animal and how it could be used. As a teacher at the ______________ Institute, he tried to teach his students all the things he learned and how to be good stewards of what had been given to them. He is, perhaps, best known for his work with peanuts.

Many southern farmers grew ___________ every year. Each year the soil lost more of the vitamins and minerals needed by the cotton ___________, so the plants were smaller and produced even less cotton. Dr. Carver encouraged the farmers to plant other crops to give the _______ a rest. Few farmers listened until the boll weevil came and ate nearly all the cotton before it could be _______________. Then all the farmers wanted to grow something else. Dr. Carver encouraged them to grow peanuts.

Now the farmers had a new problem. People did not know what to do with peanuts, so no one wanted to __________ them. Dr. Carver determined to solve this problem also. He locked himself in his _________________ with several baskets of peanuts. For days he stayed in his laboratory working. Finally he opened the __________ . He had many new products made from ______________ to show everyone. There was, of course, peanut butter as well as milk, margarine, Worcestershire sauce, rubbing oil, hand lotion, ink, glue and many other items. Everyone was amazed at all the things that could be done with a simple peanut.

He then wrote and talked to men who owned large ___________ to encourage them to use peanuts to make new products. The factories began buying lots of peanuts and the farmers' _______________ was solved.

buy	cotton	Tuskegee
factories	harvested	door
laboratory	peanuts	plants
problem	scientist	soil

For an exciting but easy to read book about George Washington Carver, go to www.summerbookcompany.com/indivbooks/bcarver.htm or call 877-684-8502.

Thursday

Divide.

7)51 8)76 6)41 3)11 5)29 9)30

5)49 7)61 8)49 4)19 9)77 2)20

Look at the graph to answer the following questions.

1. Who read the fewest books? ______________________
2. Who read more books, the boys or the girls? ______________________
3. Which two people read the same number of books? ______________________

4. How many more books did Laura read than Sandra? ______________________

Make the bold word plural and write it on the lines to make a good sentence.

wife 1. The men helped their ________________ put on their coats.

shirt 2. The store had long-sleeved ________________ on sale.

daisy 3. The children ran through the field of ________________.

calf 4. All the ________________ stayed close to their mothers during the storm.

bush 5. A row of ________________ is sometimes called a hedge.

Read the following story. Underline all the incomplete sentences.

One rainy day. Albert made a rubber band gun. From a kit. The gun was not hard to make. The gun is easy to cock and shoot. Fun shooting at a paper target. Sometimes Albert and his dad have a rubber band war. That is always lots of fun for Albert. Even if he loses.

Number each group of words in alphabetical order.

____ pine	____ yarn	____ barn	____ cab
____ pillow	____ younger	____ bring	____ car
____ penny	____ yard	____ best	____ canary
____ pony	____ yellow	____ bark	____ case
____ peony	____ yo-yo	____ bang	____ can
____ peep	____ yell	____ bill	____ call

____ head	____ joked	____ life	____ water
____ heat	____ joking	____ living	____ wait
____ hear	____ joke	____ liver	____ watt
____ heard	____ jokes	____ lift	____ waste

abcdefghijklmnopqrstuvwxyz

Circle the words that would be on the page between manager - maybe.

marble	man	mane	maple	make
mast	metal	march	male	map

Circle the words that would be on the page between bean - beverage.

beat	bead	beyond	be	bet
back	bitter	beside	best	berry
bewail	bewilder	betray	blister	bass

abcdefghijklmnopqrstuvwxyz

Write the Arabic numeral for the Roman numeral.
Remember: I = 1, V = 5, X = 10, L = 50 and C = 100.

XXV ______________ CX ______________ XLIV ______________

VIII ______________ XIV ______________ CIX ______________

XIV ______________ XVIII ______________ LXVI ______________

Solve these story problems.

1. In Owasaka County it rained 114 days last year. How many days did it not rain?

____

2. Jennifer has 24 slices of pizza. If 6 people share the pizza fairly (including Jennifer), how many slices can each person eat?

____

3. Jack was playing golf with his dad. The first hole is 425 yards long. On the first shot, Jack's ball went 230 yards. On the second shot, it went 150 yards. How many yards does Jack have left to go?

____

Underline the correct word.

1. The Jones family packed the moving truck (theirselves, themselves).
2. I think that blue jacket hanging on the hook is (hers, her's).
3. Does (your, you're) dog know any tricks?
4. (Its, It's) not hard to believe that Jesus walked on water.
5. Mother said he must clean his room (himself, hisself).

*Tell whether the pairs of words are synonyms (**syn.**), homonyms (**hom.**) or antonyms (**ant.**).*

lady, woman __________ sick, well __________ tare, tear __________

hour, our __________ dead, alive __________ damp, moist __________

new, old __________ couch, sofa __________ son, sun __________

far, distant __________ threw, through __________ right, left __________

The Tiger

from *An Alphabet of Quadrupeds*

This very beautiful animal, called a tiger, lives in India. India is a very hot country in Asia. Tigers are fierce and will often kill men and animals much larger than themselves. They live in the woods and thickets, called jungles, where men hunt them. Tigers eat the flesh of animals which they kill. We have none in America except a few kept for show. The tiger is as big as a lion and has the shape of a cat, but much larger. He has a long tail and striped skin, covered with short hair. His skin is sometimes used for decoration. He is quite active and can jump far. Some tigers have been tamed, but he is a very sly and dangerous creature. He cannot be trusted.

Answer the questions about the paragraph.

1. What do tigers eat? plants meat tiger food
2. Where do tigers normally live? the zoo America India
3. Tiger skins are used for what? ____________________
4. Why would a tiger be in the United States? ____________________
5. Write a synonym for the word *fierce.*

____

Color the tiger.

Monday

Add.

219	$4.57	514	139	$4.44	374	363
+ 89	+ 0.78	+ 59	+ 247	+ 0.85	+ 505	+ 127

Subtract to find how much change should be made. Draw coins to show the change.

Jon's dad bought lunch for $4.23. He paid $5.00.	Carol's sister bought her a scarf for $3.91. She paid $4.00.
Ann's mom bought a few groceries for $9.74. She paid $10.00.	Frank's brother bought him a belt for $5.03. He paid $5.25.

Underline all the nouns.

1. The Hubers have a small rock wall for climbing on the side of their play set.
2. The boys pretend they are mountain climbers and brave adventurers.
3. Tim and Randy have strong hands and arms from climbing the rock wall.
4. The boys grip the little ledges with their fingers and toes.
5. When they were small, the boys thought the yellow rope was a challenge.

Circle the letters that should be capitalized. Put an X on any letter that is capitalized and should not be.

1. jack london wrote *call of the wild* and *white fang*.
2. mr. J. n. barnsworth is my Uncle on my Father's side of the Family.
3. have you ever Read *on the banks of plum creek* by laura Ingalls wilder?
4. i Love to go to see my Grandmother and see all the animals on her Farm.
5. sometimes easter comes in the Month of march and sometimes in april.

Put each group of items in order from first to last or smallest to largest.

______ May
______ January
______ August
______ March
______ June

______ October
______ April
______ December
______ July
______ February

______ sunset
______ dawn
______ morning
______ afternoon
______ noon

______ word
______ chapter
______ sentence
______ book
______ paragraph

______ roll over
______ run
______ crawl
______ walk
______ sit up

______ Tuesday
______ Saturday
______ Wednesday
______ Thursday
______ Monday

______ preschool
______ elementary school
______ kindergarten
______ high school
______ college

______ grit
______ boulder
______ pebble
______ mountain
______ stone

______ acorn
______ lumber
______ sapling
______ chair
______ tree

Tuesday

Multiply.

0	9	3	4	8	12	35	56	71	97
x 7	x 6	x 3	x 0	x 10	x 2	x 9	x 8	x 7	x 4

Draw a rectangle and color the correct amount.

$\frac{1}{3}$ $\frac{3}{4}$ $\frac{5}{6}$

$\frac{2}{5}$ $\frac{1}{2}$ $\frac{1}{4}$

Put periods where they belong.

1. The President of the United States lives in Washington, D C
2. She lives on the corner of Pine St and Cherry Rd
3. Dr H G Benson is our family's dentist
4. Mon is the day my mother does the laundry, and Thurs is the day she shops
5. Mr and Mrs Thompson live four blocks away on Vine St

Underline the adjectives in the sentences and draw an arrow to the word it describes.

1. Henry's blue aluminum bat is everyone's favorite.
2. The neighborhood boys play on a team with their dads.
3. This year the team bought new bases for the baseball diamond.
4. The dads mow the green grass and the boys smooth the brown dirt.
5. The mothers and their daughters provide cold drinks and yummy snacks.

??? If you add up the ages of everyone in your family will it equal more than 100?

Encyclopedias have many articles and provide much information. The articles are arranged in alphabetical order. Read the article below and answer the questions.

Marshmallows Marshmallows were first made from a plant that grew wild in marshes. It was called the mallow plant. Egyptians discovered the process of making this plant into a gooey treat. They used the sap from the plant and mixed nuts and honey with it.

Many years later the French decided to whip the sap by hand to make it fluffy. They also added cornstarch to make it stiff. They sold the treat in their candy stores. This process took a lot of time to do by hand. Candy makers started searching for an easier way to make marshmallows. Instead of using the mallow plant, candy makers began using gelatin, and America learned about the special treat.

A man named Alex Doumak made some more changes to the process. Marshmallow goo was put through tubes and then cut into pieces. Marshmallows became more popular and many people used them in different recipes.

Today Americans buy more marshmallows than any other country in the world. They buy more than ninety million pounds every year! The same ingredients - gelatin, corn syrup, starch, sugar and water - can be combined at home to make marshmallows. Salt and vanilla can be added for flavoring.

Answer the questions about the encyclopedia article.

1. What is the name of the plant from which marshmallows were first made?

   papyrus   mallow   sap   candy

2. What was the first country to make marshmallows?________________________

3. Using digits, write the number of pounds of marshmallows that Americans buy every year.

   ____

4. Would the entry for marshmallows come before or after an entry on the month of

   March?   before   after

5. Number the words in the order you could find them in the encyclopedia.

   ___ gelatin   ____ candy   ____ cornstarch   ____ vanilla   ____ sugar

6. Marshmallows could be found between which two entries?

   Maryland - Mice   Marborough - Mexico   Miracle - Miranda

Subtract.

603	977	530	721	874	543	635	714
- 353	- 266	- 307	- 188	- 479	- 167	- 48	- 275

Use the numbers to make four math facts.

3 18 6	6 48 8	5 20 4
____ x ____ = ____	____ x ____ = ____	____ x ____ = ____
____ x ____ = ____	____ x ____ = ____	____ x ____ = ____
____ ÷ ____ = ____	____ ÷ ____ = ____	____ ÷ ____ = ____
____ ÷ ____ = ____	____ ÷ ____ = ____	____ ÷ ____ = ____

Solve this story problem.

1. The Incredible Toy Palace has 194 stuffed animals, 217 dolls and 423 balls. How many of these three toys do they have?

____

Tell whether the sentence is **declarative, interrogative,** *or* **exclamatory***.*

________________ 1. Watch out for that hornet's nest!

________________ 2. Do you know how hot it is outside?

________________ 3. I like chocolate ice cream better than strawberry ice cream.

________________ 4. Where is the dog?

________________ 5. Matt will be going into the fourth grade next year.

Put commas where they belong.

1. Mountain bikes dirt bikes and speed bikes are all fun to ride.
2. Mike hopped on his bike rode over to the store and bought some sugar.
3. Yes I really like the way you cleaned your bicycle and polished it.
4. Megan you must wear a bicycle helmet when you ride your bike on the street.

Summer Adventure

Have your parents help you find an old road or path near your town and take a bike hike with them. Offer to help pack and carry a picnic lunch for everyone.

Circle the words and phrases that describe insects.

four legs	two body parts	have bones	have feathers
have fur	many teeth	long hair	eight legs
have gills	six legs	have antennae	most can fly
lay eggs	babies drink milk	three body parts	have one eye

Circle the creatures that are insects.

Divide.

0 ÷ 8 = ______ 10 ÷ 2 = ______ 1 ÷ 1 = ______ 24 ÷ 3 = ______

8 ÷ 2 = ______ 32 ÷ 8 = ______ 0 ÷ 3 = ______ 28 ÷ 4 = ______

6 ÷ 1 = ______ 20 ÷ 5 = ______ 6 ÷ 2 = ______ 63 ÷ 7 = ______

Add.

19	285	92	331	596	38	482	33
22	555	73	468	371	15	298	57
+ 88	+ 127	+ 24	+ 229	+ 144	+ 41	+ 346	+ 13

Write the plural of each word on the line.

wrench ____________ child ____________ car ____________

fish ____________ wife ____________ shelf ____________

lady ____________ penny ____________ man ____________

wish ____________ deer ____________ field ____________

Look each word up in the dictionary. Copy the first definition onto the lines.

allegiance - ____

____

deaf - ____

____

target - ____

____

scrub - ____

____

Write the homonyms in the crossword puzzle.

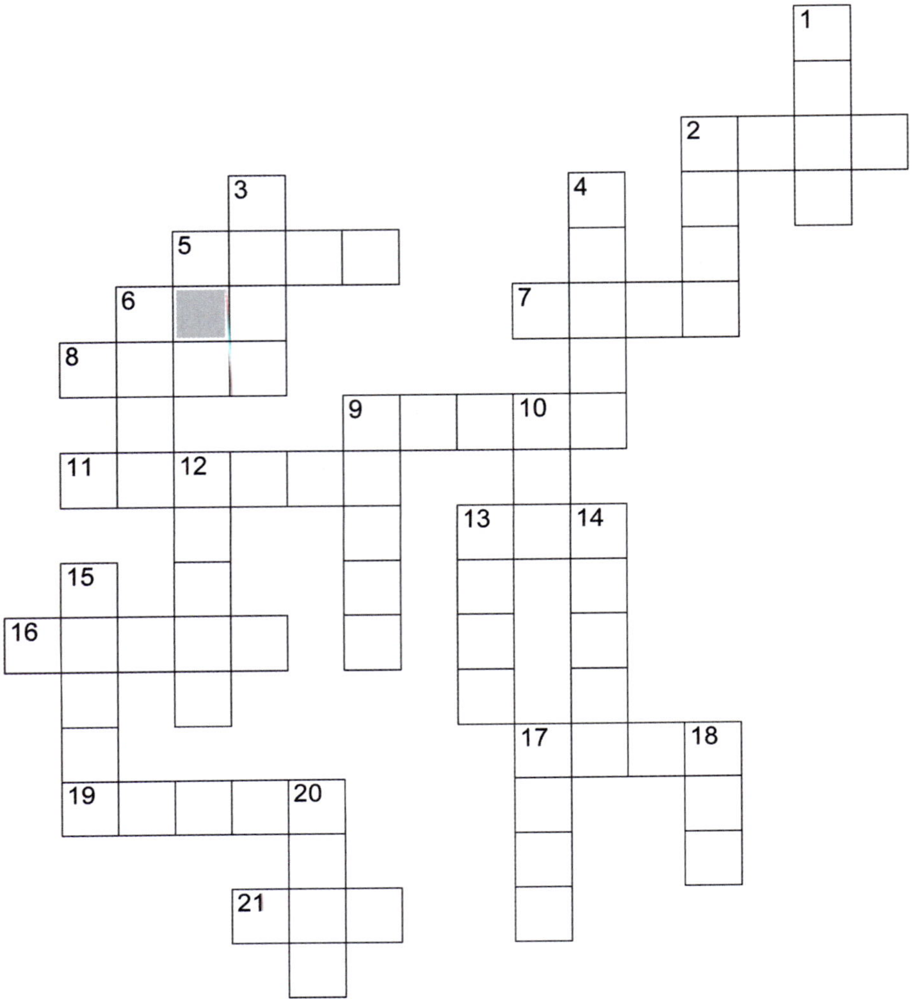

Across
2. prey
5. weight
7. here
8. male
9. waste
11. slay
13. do
16. knight
17. meat
19. there
21. won

Down
1. bare
2. pair
3. tale
4. grate
6. pale
9. wail
10. sea
12. ate
13. dear
14. wear
15. write
17. mane
18. too
20. wring

Underline the number in the tens place and circle the number in the thousands place.

32	46,875	129	5,034,872
7,205	19,634	90	5
1,681,304	9	586	739,530

Solve these story problems.

1. Dee bought six pizzas that were each $8.50 for a party. If she gave the delivery man $55.00, how much change should she get?

____

2. Virginia has two fruit pies to serve for dessert after dinner. If there are twelve people for dinner, into how many slices will she need to cut each pie?

____

3. The Terrific Tree Trimmer Company has trimmed 32 trees a week for the last 3 weeks. How many trees have they trimmed in the last 3 weeks?

____

Put quotation marks where they belong.

Men, said the coach, We will be playing a very good team on Saturday, but I think we are ready for them.

After practice Barry said to Joseph, We did not do very well against this team last year.

I know, replied Joseph, but the coach seems to think we will do better this year.

Circle possessive words (words that show ownership).

1. Is that Barry's soccer ball, or is it Henry's?
2. The man's new suit is gray, and the woman's coat is black.
3. The police sped after the man who took the lady's purse.
4. The tree house in the backyard is Gary's and Tim's special creation.
5. The pet store's dogs include four poodles and three cocker spaniels.

A Bear Story
by Edgar A. Guest

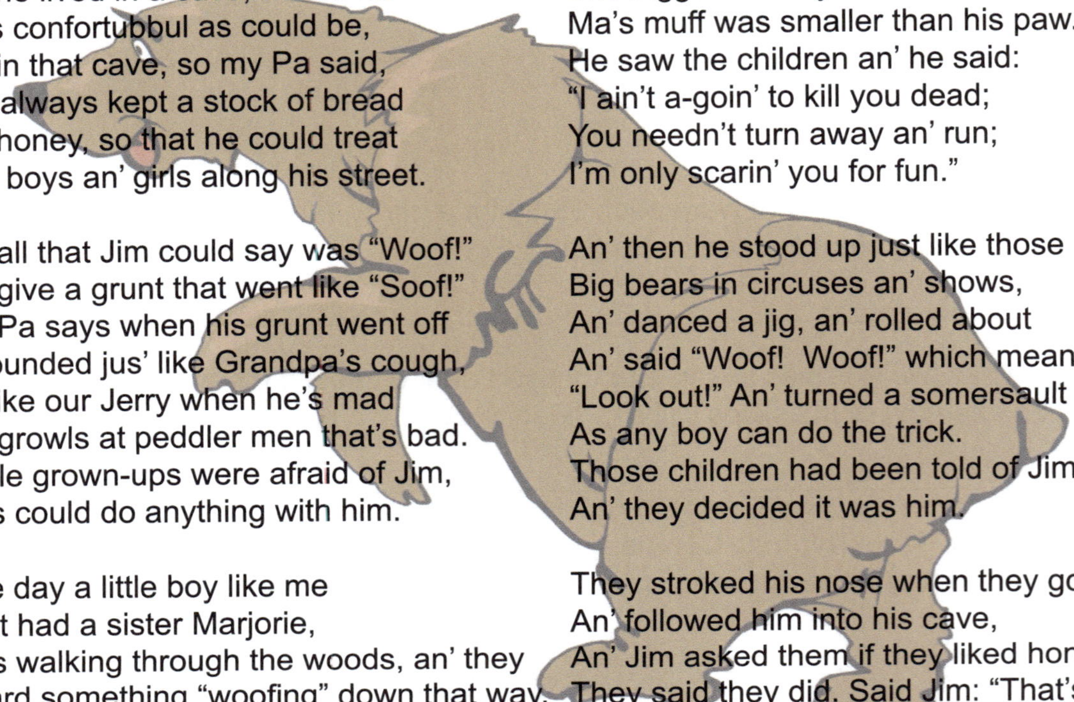

There was a bear -- his name was Jim,
An' children weren't askeered of him,
An' he lived in a cave, where he
Was confortubbul as could be,
An' in that cave, so my Pa said,
Jim always kept a stock of bread
An' honey, so that he could treat
The boys an' girls along his street.

An' all that Jim could say was "Woof!"
An' give a grunt that went like "Soof!"
An' Pa says when his grunt went off
It sounded jus' like Grandpa's cough,
Or like our Jerry when he's mad
An' growls at peddler men that's bad.
While grown-ups were afraid of Jim,
Kids could do anything with him.

One day a little boy like me
That had a sister Marjorie,
Was walking through the woods, an' they
Heard something "woofing" down that way,
An' they was scared an' stood stock still
An' wished they had a gun to kill
Whatever 'twas, but little boys
Don't have no guns that make a noise.

An' soon the "woofing" closer grew,
An' then a bear came into view,
The biggest bear you ever saw --
Ma's muff was smaller than his paw.
He saw the children an' he said:
"I ain't a-goin' to kill you dead;
You needn't turn away an' run;
I'm only scarin' you for fun."

An' then he stood up just like those
Big bears in circuses an' shows,
An' danced a jig, an' rolled about
An' said "Woof! Woof!" which meant
"Look out!" An' turned a somersault as slick
As any boy can do the trick.
Those children had been told of Jim
An' they decided it was him.

They stroked his nose when they got brave,
An' followed him into his cave,
An' Jim asked them if they liked honey,
They said they did. Said Jim: "That's funny.
I've asked a thousand boys or so
That question, an' not one's said no."
What happened then I cannot say
'Cause next I knew 'twas light as day.

Answer the questions about the poem.

1. In the first verse, *askeered* is what real word? ______________________________

2. How should *confortubbul* be spelled? ______________________________________

3. How do you know that this story is not true? ______________________________

____

Add.

59	13	60	73	41	18	55	88	31	93
+ 6	+ 96	+ 48	+ 27	+ 79	+ 1	+ 36	+ 22	+ 66	+ 15

Use each set of numbers to make four math facts.

7 16 9	8 14 6	5 12 7
____ + ____ = ____	____ + ____ = ____	____ + ____ = ____
____ + ____ = ____	____ + ____ = ____	____ + ____ = ____
____ - ____ = ____	____ - ____ = ____	____ - ____ = ____
____ - ____ = ____	____ - ____ = ____	____ - ____ = ____

Underline all the nouns.

Owls are excellent hunters for several reasons. First they have large eyes that see better than a human's eyes. They cannot turn their eyes in their heads the way people can, so they turn their necks. Owls also have special feathers on their wings which help the owls to fly almost silently. The feet of an owl are very strong and have sharp claws. All these things help make an owl a very good hunter.

Cross out the letters that should be capitalized and write a capital letter over them.

1. larry and his dad built a super ten rocket from a kit.
2. last saturday they went to a field at mentrose park and launched the rocket.
3. larry was impressed by how high it went.
4. dad was quite pleased with how well larry had followed the directions when he built the rocket.
5. next larry and his dad plan to build a wonder winger later this summer.

☺ Something Extra ☺

On a separate page, write at least five good sentences telling about a vacation you have taken this summer. If you haven't been on vacation yet, write about a vacation you would like to take.

Choose the operation or operations you would need to do to find the answer. You do not have to solve the problems unless you want to for extra practice.

1. Frank can put on a horse shoe in eighteen minutes. If a man has a team of four horses that all need new shoes, how long will it take Frank to finish them all?

Step 1: add subtract multiply divide

Step 2: add subtract multiply divide

2. Frank charges $75 to shoe a horse. How much is that per hoof?

add subtract multiply divide

3. Frank's brother, Fred, is just learning to shoe horses. It takes him five minutes more per hoof than it takes Frank. How much longer does it take Fred to shoe a horse?

add subtract multiply divide

4. Horse shoes cost Frank $4.75 each, but he charges his customers $5.50. How much money is Frank making on each shoe?

add subtract multiply divide

5. Frank charged Mr. Hodgekins $75 to shoe his horse and $5.50 each for four extra horse shoes. How much did Mr. Hodgekins owe?

Step 1: add subtract multiply divide

Step 2: add subtract multiply divide

6. All the horses in the Arabian Club were brought to Frank for new shoes before they were in the parade. Frank worked extra fast and finished a horse every seventy minutes. If he worked for five hours straight, how many horses did he completely finish?

Step 1: add subtract multiply divide

Step 2: add subtract multiply divide

7. Frank ordered thirty-six small shoes, eighty-four medium shoes, and sixteen large shoes. How many shoes did he order in all?

add subtract multiply divide

8. Frank is forty-eight years old and has been in business for twenty-seven years. He hopes to retire when he is sixty-five. How many more years will he be working?

add subtract multiply divide

Multiply.

2 x 0 = ______ 9 x 7 = ______ 3 x 7 = ______ 1 x 4 = ______

6 x 10 = ______ 5 x 8 = ______ 4 x 9 = ______ 7 x 6 = ______

10 x 5 = ______ 8 x 3 = ______ 10 x 2 = ______ 0 x 1 = ______

Write the correct fraction on the line.

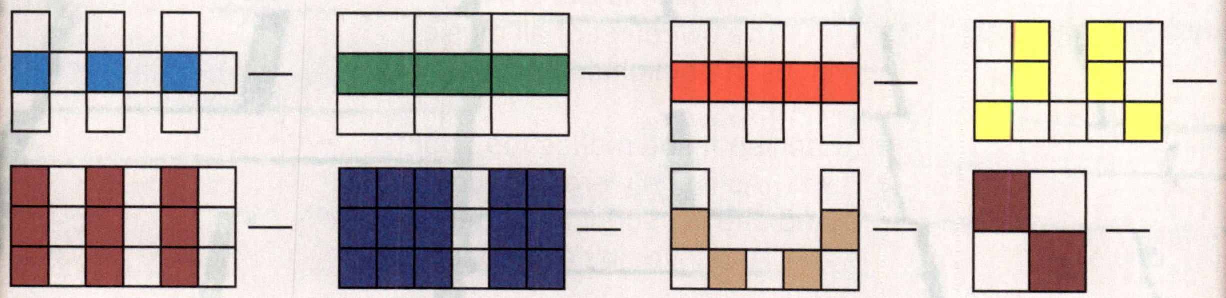

Circle all the adjectives.

1. That pink, flowered couch does not match the orange, striped curtains.
2. The new curtains in Sarah's room have white lace around the edges.
3. Mr. Jacobs has a big, shiny, new truck that he washes every Saturday.
4. Those black and white penguins surely do look cute.
5. The bride had a lacy, white dress and flowered veil.

Insert the missing periods and capital letters.

last may t j and chad got a super bouncy ball as a gift they like to bounce it back and forth to each other when they bounce it on the brick sidewalk, the uneven bricks cause the ball to bounce in strange ways t j likes to see if he can bounce the ball right past chad

Cheerfulness
by Marian Douglas

There is a little maiden -
Who is she? Do you know?
Who always has a welcome,
Wherever she may go.

Her face is like the May time,
Her voice is like a bird's;
The sweetest of all music
Is in her lightsome words.

Each spot she makes the brighter,
As if she were the sun;
And she is sought and cherished
And loved by everyone;

By old folks and by children,
By lofty and by low:
Who is this little maiden?
Does anybody know?

You surely must have met her.
You certainly can guess;
What! I must introduce her?
Her name is Cheerfulness.

Answer the questions about the poem.

1. What is a maiden? a boy a girl an animal
2. Is this poem describing a particular girl named Cheerfulness? yes no

   Who is this poem describing? ____________________________________
3. Why do people like her so much? ____________________________________
4. What does *cherished* mean? ____________________________________
5. Could this poem be describing you today? yes no

Subtract.

$67.59	1,895	3,362	$77.58	4,579	4,015	$86.73
- 8.38	- 226	- 484	- 1.51	- 656	- 890	- 4.31

*Put **<** or **>** in the circle.*

3 + 2 ◯ 4 + 2	9 x 2 ◯ 3 x 7	7 + 0 ◯ 8 + 2	4 x 6 ◯ 9 x 6
8 + 7 ◯ 5 + 9	7 x 7 ◯ 9 x 3	7 + 4 ◯ 2 + 8	3 x 7 ◯ 6 x 6
0 + 5 ◯ 2 + 2	3 x 8 ◯ 5 x 5	6 + 3 ◯ 9 + 4	8 x 7 ◯ 8 x 9

Circle the words that show ownership. Underline the verbs.

The twins, Sam and Dan, built a small reading loft in a tree. Sam's favorite time of day for reading is in the morning. Dan's favorite time is in the late afternoon. The boys' parents are glad that Sam and Dan like books.

The boys' loft is used for other things besides reading. It is Sam's favorite lookout when playing army. The high loft is Dan's best perch when using his binoculars.

Place commas where they belong.

1. Thomas please do not let your wet umbrella drip on the carpet.
2. Susan's aunt lives in Grafton WV.
3. Billy I need you to mow the lawn clean your room and take out the trash.
4. The Declaration of Independence was signed in Philadelphia PA.
5. Beans peas carrots and beets are all vegetables.

Write the two words for these contractions.

couldn't ______________________ you've ______________________

I'm ______________________ she'll ______________________

we're ______________________ it's ______________________

they're ______________________ you'd ______________________

Cross out the item in each row that does not belong. Then tell why the other items belong together.

Example: candy apple stop sign ~~the ocean~~ fire engine
Why? The other items are usually red.

1. markers crayons scissors pencil

   Why? ______________________________

2. gerbil cat mouse hamster

   Why? ______________________________

3. swimming canoeing rafting hiking

   Why? ______________________________

4. baby mother infant newborn

   Why? ______________________________

5. big large huge round

   Why? ______________________________

6. Paul Peter Priscilla Patrick

   Why? ______________________________

7. mittens hat hood cap

   Why? ______________________________

8. stove oven mixer microwave

   Why? ______________________________

9. mane scales tail hoof

   Why? ______________________________

10. quickly slowly neatly tired

    Why? ______________________________

Divide.

0 ÷ 8 = ______ 10 ÷ 2 = ______ 1 ÷ 1 = ______ 24 ÷ 3 = ______

8 ÷ 2 = ______ 32 ÷ 8 = ______ 0 ÷ 3 = ______ 28 ÷ 4 = ______

6 ÷ 1 = ______ 20 ÷ 5 = ______ 6 ÷ 2 = ______ 63 ÷ 7 = ______

Fill in the blanks.

36 inches = ______ feet 2 yards = ______ feet 3 yards = ______ feet

9 feet = ______ yards 6 feet = ______ yards 2 feet = ______ inches

24 inches = ______ feet 3 feet = ______ inches 1 yard = ______ inches

Write the plural form of the word on the line.

moose ________________ daddy ________________ truck ________________

leaf ________________ sheep ________________ ax ________________

arm ________________ church ________________ bush ________________

pass ________________ nail ________________ reply ________________

Write **complete** *on the line if the words make a complete sentence. Write* **incomplete** *if the words do not make a complete sentence.*

________________ 1. A pool of cool, sparkling water.

________________ 2. Jim can swim like a fish.

________________ 3. Splashing and playing together.

________________ 4. Shannon dives very well.

________________ 5. Relief from summer heat.

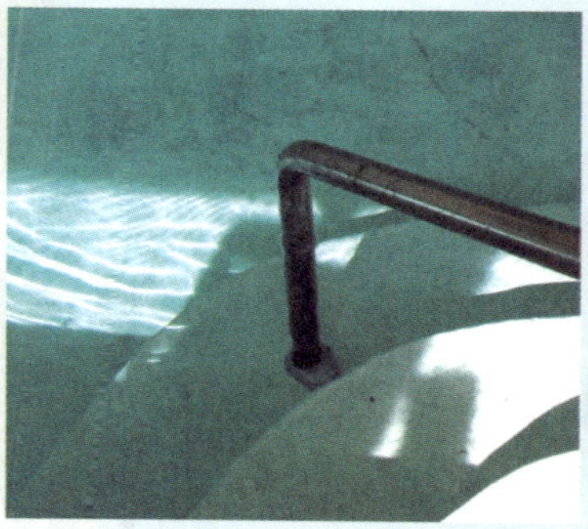

Something Special

Time is the most precious thing a person has. Give some of your time to someone else today by helping them do a job more quickly.

Hint Hunter

Five neighbors on Valley View Road have different jobs in the community. Mr. Hardy's job is extremely noisy, so he wears ear plugs every day. Mr. Lawson has helped with the evening news every week night for the last twelve years. Mr. Eavers really enjoys his job. He loves the rush and hurry and the chance to save lives and property. He trains carefully all the time, so he will not get hurt in dangerous situations. Mr. Finch started learning his trade when he was a boy helping his dad. He thinks helping to build homes for other people is a really special job. Mr. Green's favorite time of day is when he gets to help children cross the street after school. Which man has which job?

Mr. Eavers 

Mr. Finch 

Mr. Greene 

Mr. Hardy 

Mr. Lawson 

Friday

Fill in the missing numbers.

5 + _____ = 10	9 x _____ = 63	7 + _____ = 16	8 x _____ = 40
6 + _____ = 12	7 x _____ = 56	6 + _____ = 15	6 x _____ = 30
9 + _____ = 16	5 x _____ = 40	7 + _____ = 13	6 x _____ = 42

Solve these story problems.

1. Farmer Joe has to deliver 8 dozen eggs to his customers today. How many eggs will he be delivering?

____

2. Laura has 23 paper dolls and Michelle has 17. How many more does Laura have?

____

3. Ben has 14 conch shells, 12 clam shells and 18 periwinkle shells in his shell collection. How many shells does he have altogether?

____

Write a homonym on the line for the bold word.

wait 1. When you stand on a scale, it tells you your _______________.

hair 2. A _______________ is another name for a rabbit.

so 3. A tailor is a man who will _______________ for money.

new 4. Andrea _______________ the answers to all the questions on the test.

knight 5. It is quite dark at ____________________.

Circle the correct word or words.

1. Do you believe (there is, there are) a dog who can write?
2. I think he (has, have) finished his chores cheerfully.
3. (There is, There are) several low swings on the swing set.
4. The swing set (are, is) one of the favorite places for children to play on the playground.
5. Do you know how many stars (there is, there are) in the sky?

What is the best piece of playground equipment you have ever played on in your whole life? ____________________________

Little Goody Two Shoes
Adapted from *Goldsmith*

Margery's parents had died. She and her brother were very poor and ragged. Though Tommy had two shoes, Margery had only one. They had nothing, poor little things, but what kind people gave to them. Each night they lay on hay in a barn.

Mr. Smith was a very good man. Although he was poor, he took the children home to live with him. Mr. Smith had a friend who was a wealthy man. When he heard about Margery and Tommy, this man gave Mr. Smith some money. It was to buy Margery a new pair of shoes and Tommy a new suit of clothes.

The next morning the shoemaker came in with Margery's new shoes. She put them on in great glee and ran out to Mrs. Smith. Margery cried, "Two shoes, two shoes. Goody, two shoes!" She did this to all the people she met, so that soon she was known far and wide as Goody Two Shoes.

Dear little Margery saw how good and wise Mr. Smith was. She thought it was because he read so many books. Margery wished so badly to learn to read. She would borrow books from the school children and sit down and read and read. Very soon she could read better than any of her playmates.

Margery enjoyed her books so much that she wished everybody else could read too, so she formed a plan.

First, she made letters out of bits of wood with her knife. She worked and worked until there were ten sets of small letters and six sets of the big letters. She then made the little tots spell words with her wooden letters. Each morning, with her basket full of wooden letters, Margery went around from house to house. The little children learned to read very quickly.

At last Margery grew up and was given a real school to teach. She still used her little wooden letters and made the children use them to spell the words.

Another gentleman, Sir Charles Jones heard of Margery's goodness. He offered her a home if she would teach his daughter. In fact he finally fell in love with Margery, and they were married in a big church.

She did not forget the children, you may be sure. A house in the village was fitted up as a school, and all the boys and girls were taught to read and write.

Answer the questions about the story.

1. Why were Margery and her brother all alone in the world? ______________________
____

2. At the beginning of the story, Margery had how many shoes? 0 1 2

3. Margery believed the Mr. Smith was wise because he did what?
____

4. How many sets of letters did she make altogether? 6 10 16 26

5. Do you think the children enjoyed learning from Margery? yes no

   Why?____

6. Why is this story called "Little Goody Two Shoes"? ______________________
____

Add.

245	547	167	588	379	238	328
+ 365	+ 225	+ 439	+ 254	+ 474	+ 158	+ 486

Subtract to find how much change should be made. Draw coins to show the change.

Mark owes Peter $2.15. He gave him $2.25.	Kathy owes Ginger $0.40. She gave her $0.50.
Laura owes Danielle $1.70. She gave her two dollars.	Tim owes Robert $8.13. He gave him $8.25.

Circle the letters that should be capitalized.

1. is aunt hilary's birthday in september or october?
2. mr. b. f. kepler and mrs. d. n. hardison are brother and sister.
3. on our vacation we are going to visit jamestown and yorktown, virginia.
4. does riverside lane actually run right along the side of black lick river?
5. my dad thinks my mom is the most wonderful woman in the world.

Put a ✓ over the underlined word if it is a noun. Put an **X** *over the word if it is not a noun.*

Randall loves his skateboard. He has learned to do several tricks on it. When Randall first started using his skateboard, he often forgot to wear his helmet, knee pads and elbow pads. After falling down and getting all scraped up a few times, Randall realized it was important to wear his safety gear whenever he was using his skateboard.

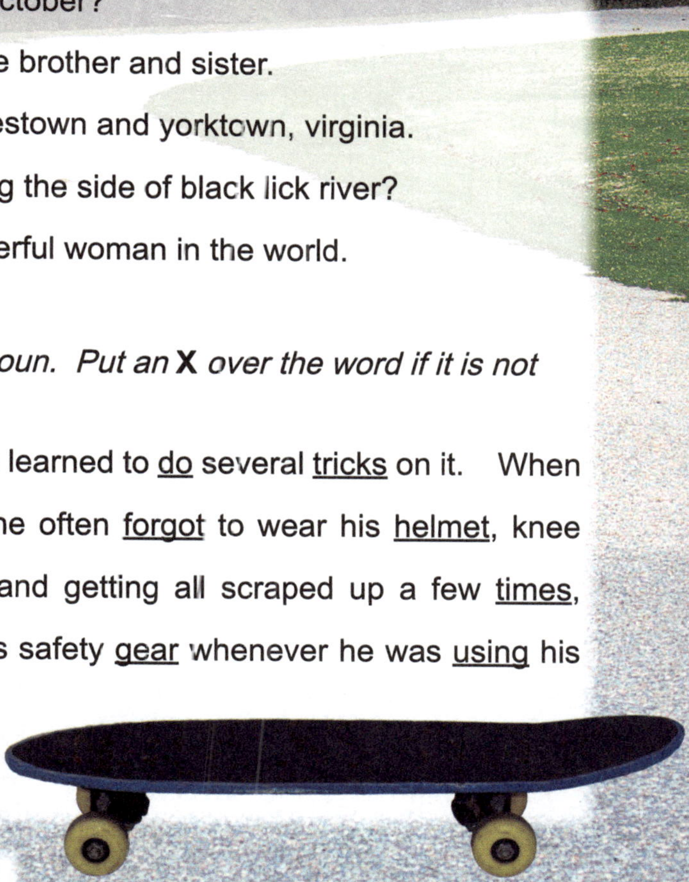

Answer the questions about the map.

1. After each state, write its letter from the map.

California _______	Oklahoma _______
Florida _______	Pennsylvania _______
Georgia _______	Texas _______
Michigan _______	Virginia _______
Montana _______	Washington _______

2. Name two states that border the Atlantic Ocean. ____________________________

3. Name two states that border Canada. ____________________________

4. Name two states that border the Pacific Ocean. ____________________________

____

Tuesday

Multiply.

10	4	1	7	9	3	22	45	68	86
x 6	x 3	x 5	x 7	x 10	x 9	x 8	x 4	x 2	x 1

Color in the circles.

○ ○ $1\frac{1}{4}$

○ ○ ○ $2\frac{1}{2}$

○ ○ ○ $2\frac{3}{4}$

○ ○ ○ ○ $1\frac{2}{3}$

Place periods and capital letters where they belong in the paragraph.

on a rainy day, a paddle and ball is a good toy you can play several different games with it you can try to catch the ball in all the holes in order for another game, you and a brother or sister can pick a number and see who reaches it first if you use your imagination, you can think of all kinds of fun things to do with a ball and a paddle

Write an adjective before each word to describe it. Try not to use the same word twice.

______________ bird	______________ house	______________ girl
______________ car	______________ boy	______________ dish
______________ apple	______________ man	______________ tree
______________ bed	______________ cat	______________ pen

Use the information below to answer the questions.

Carl's Camping **If we don't have it, you don't need it!**

Two Man Tent - Quality lightweight tent easily sets up at night. Extra waterproof floor. Green or brown. **$68.98**

Family Tent - This great tent is so high even dad can stand up inside. Sleeps 6. **$95.99**
Extra rain cover **$24.95**

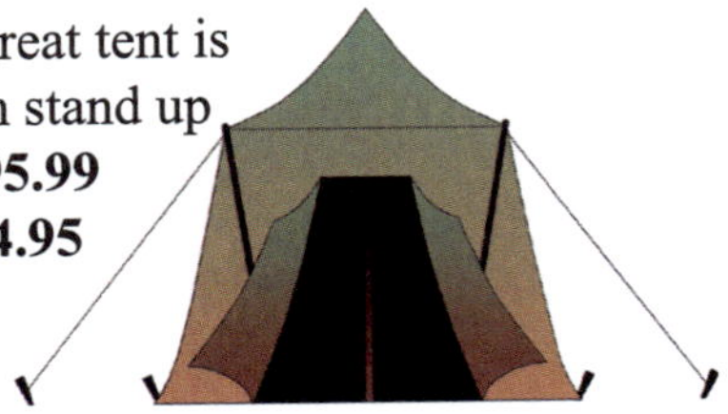

Bright Lantern . . **$17.25**
Firewood Ax **$15.85**
Super Shovel . . . **$12.45**

Three Tool Set . . .**$35.95**

Carry all your gear in this sturdy back pack. The bedroll will keep you warm even on cold nights.
Backpack **$31.49**
Bedroll **$19.88**
Backpack and Bedroll . **$49.50**

1. How much is the family tent with the rain cover?

2. Thomas paid $90 when he bought the two-man tent and the lantern. How much change did he receive?

3. How much more is it if you buy the lantern, ax, and shovel separately than if you buy the three piece tool set?

4. All twelve of the boys in the Super Scout Club wanted to buy a backpack and bedroll set before the club's next camping trip. Mr. Carl, the owner, said he would give each boy a $5 coupon. How much is a backpack and bedroll set when a boy uses his coupon?

5. If all twelve boys use their coupons, how much money will they save?

6. Mr. Pennly saw an ad in the paper saying that he could save $10 if he bought the family tent and the three piece tool set on Saturday. What would be the total for those items on Saturday?

Wednesday

Subtract and check by adding.

60		82		68		95	
- 24	+ 24	- 15	+ 15	- 29	+ 29	- 17	+ 17

Use the numbers to make four equations.

7 63 9

____ x ____ = ____
____ x ____ = ____
____ ÷ ____ = ____
____ ÷ ____ = ____

8 56 7

____ x ____ = ____
____ x ____ = ____
____ ÷ ____ = ____
____ ÷ ____ = ____

5 30 6

____ x ____ = ____
____ x ____ = ____
____ ÷ ____ = ____
____ ÷ ____ = ____

Write the type of sentence called for by the bold word.

declarative ____

exclamatory ____

interrogative ____

Place commas where they belong.

1. Marcie's father was born on July 24 1962 in Chicago.
2. Yes Calvin you may ride your bike in the driveway.
3. No Dr. Barton is not in the office right now.
4. On October 12 2018 Mrs. Elliot will be one hundred years old.
5. Leigh will you please call Mrs. Fisher and see if she is ready to leave?

Underline the subject once and the verb twice.

1. After the ball game was over, my family went to a restaurant for dinner.
2. During dinner, we celebrated my brother's home run.
3. My brother's team, the Parrots, has not had a winning season.
4. Have you ever hit a home run?

Draw a line from Beethoven to his instrument, the piano. Do not go "through" any other instrument to get there.

Divide.

$6\overline{)53}$ $10\overline{)64}$ $3\overline{)7}$ $5\overline{)18}$ $2\overline{)2}$ $8\overline{)29}$

$3\overline{)17}$ $5\overline{)38}$ $10\overline{)21}$ $9\overline{)40}$ $10\overline{)75}$ $7\overline{)24}$

Look at the graph to answer the questions.

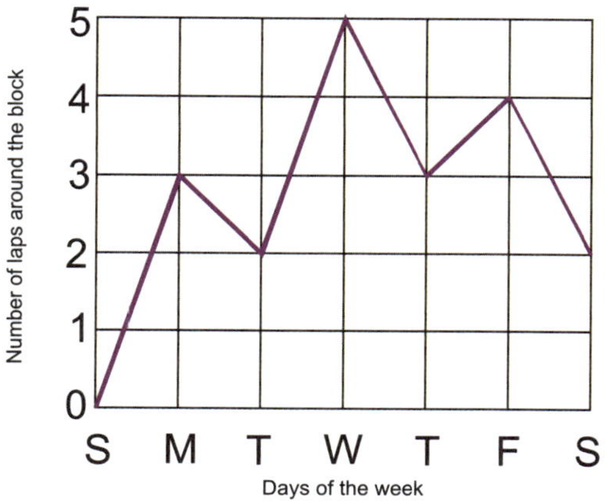

1. Which day did Michael run the most laps?

____

2. Did he run more laps Mon.-Wed. or Thurs.-Sat.?

____

3. Which day did he run the same number of laps as he ran on Monday?

____

4. Which day of the week did Michael rest? _______________________

5. How many laps did Michael run during the whole week? _______________

Number the words in each column in alphabetical order.

____ rope
____ road
____ roam
____ rode

____ jump
____ just
____ jacks
____ jail

____ skip
____ sing
____ scrap
____ step

____ hop
____ help
____ handle
____ hurry

Write the plural form of the words on the lines.

knife ______________ woman ______________ fish ______________

puppy ______________ ash ______________ ditch ______________

airplane ______________ plate ______________ goose ______________

elf ______________ city ______________ sheep ______________

Follow the directions to change one word into another.

summertime

1. Change each *e* to an *a*. __________________________

2. Change each *m* to a *v*. __________________________

3. Switch the last two letters. __________________________

4. Delete the *s*. __________________________

5. Change the *u* to an *o*. __________________________

6. Switch the *o* and the last *a*. __________________________

7. Change the last *v* to an *n*. __________________________

8. Change the *r* to a *c*. __________________________

9. Put the first *a* after the *c*. __________________________

10. Delete the first letter. __________________________

Draw a picture of the answer.

Friday

Fill in the missing numbers. Example: If 4 + 7 = 11, then 7 + 4 = 11.

If 7 + 5 = 12, then ___ + ___ = 12 — If 8 x 7 = 56, then ___ x ___ = 56

If 6 + 8 = 14, then ___ + ___ = 14 — If 5 x 3 = 15, then ___ x ___ = 15

If 2 + 9 = 11, then ___ + ___ = 11 — If 6 x 4 = 24, then ___ x ___ = 24

Solve these story problems.

1. Mr. Pine grew 47 tomatoes last year, and Mr. Ed grew 39. How many more did Mr. Pine grow?

____

2. The Saluda River is 2 times as long as the Pee Dee River which is 34 miles long. The Pee Dee River is 27 feet wide, but the Saluda River is only 24 feet wide. How long is the Saluda River?

____

Put quotation marks where they belong in the sentences.

What kind of kite is that, Carl? asked Samuel. I have never seen one like it.

I don't know what the name of it is, but Dad and I built it from straws, string, and tissue paper, replied Carl. Let me show you how well it flies!

Underline the verb(s). Circle the subject(s).

1. Wednesday is the day before Thursday.
2. That parrot talks and squawks all day.
3. Do you know where the boxes were placed?
4. Penny and Polly are identical twins.
5. Will you wash the car for me, Frank?

Extra Project

Can you look at the picture and figure out how to build a kite like this one?

The Bear and the Children

from *McGuffey's Second Eclectic Reader*

In the parlor of an inn in a small town, sat a man who had been going around with a bear. He was waiting for his supper, and the bear was tied up in the yard.

Up in the attic, three little children were playing together. The oldest might have been six years old. The youngest was not more than two.

Stump! Stump! Stump! Someone was coming up the stairs. The door flew open suddenly, and there stood the great, shaggy bear. He had gotten tired of waiting and had found his way to the stairs.

The children were badly frightened. Each one crept into a corner, but the bear found them all, smelled their clothes, and did not hurt them. "This must be a great dog," they said, and they began to pat him.

Then the bear lay down on the floor. The youngest boy climbed on his back, hid his head in the shaggy fur, and played "hide and seek."

When the oldest boy took his drum and began to strike it, then the bear rose on his hind legs and danced. At that the children gave a merry shout.

The two younger boys took their wooden guns, and gave the bear one. Away they all marched around the room.

Now the frightened mother of the children came to the door. But the youngest boy shouted joyfully. "See, we are playing soldiers!"

Then the bear's master came running up, and took the bear away.

Answer the questions about the story.

1. What do you think you would have done if you were one of the children? ________

____

____

____

____

2. Write a synonym for the word *merry*. ______________________

3. What do you think your mother would have done if she were the mother in the story?

____

____

____

Add.

455	$5.38	194	299	$5.34	164	276
+ 216	+ 0.97	+ 329	+ 425	+ 3.07	+ 418	+ 567

Use each set of numbers to make four math facts.

9 14 5	6 11 5	4 12 8
___ + ___ = ___	___ + ___ = ___	___ + ___ = ___
___ + ___ = ___	___ + ___ = ___	___ + ___ = ___
___ - ___ = ___	___ - ___ = ___	___ - ___ = ___
___ - ___ = ___	___ - ___ = ___	___ - ___ = ___

What comes next?

8, 16, ______, ______, ______, ______, ______, ______, ______

9, 18, ______, ______, ______, ______, ______, ______, ______

Circle all the nouns.

Whales are not fish. They are mammals. Fish breathe through gills, but whales breathe through a hole on the top of their heads. Fish are covered with scales. Whales are not covered with scales, but skin. Whales do not lay eggs like fish. Instead their babies are born the same way that kittens and puppies are born.

Correct the capitalization.

1. robert h. goddard is considered to be “the father of modern rocketry.”
2. the saturn rocket was used to launch the moon-going astronauts.
3. mr. paul timmons is the president of our local rocket club.
4. i like to hear mr. timmons talk about his model rockets.
5. every month, on the second saturday, the gainesville rocket club meets to launch rockets if it is not raining.

Make a new word and write it on the line. There may be more than one word that can be made from the letters. Any good word is a fine answer.

1. bird - d = ______________________________

2. fail + r = ______________________________

3. gush - s = ______________________________

4. leaf + r = ______________________________

5. meat - m = ______________________________

6. earth + s - h = ______________________________

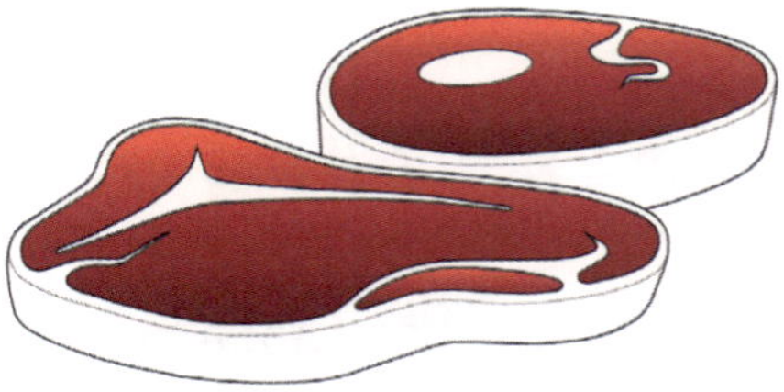

7. heel - e + d = ______________________________

8. absurd + i - u = ______________________________

9. word + a - o = ______________________________

10. smear - m + w = ______________________________

11. kidney + l - y = ______________________________

12. tours - s + e = ______________________________

Tuesday

Multiply.

1 x 0 = _____	8 x 5 = _____	10 x 9 = _____	6 x 3 = _____
2 x 10 = _____	9 x 8 = _____	5 x 6 = _____	3 x 4 = _____
7 x 2 = _____	4 x 1 = _____	0 x 3 = _____	7 x 0 = _____

Write the fraction on the line.

 ___

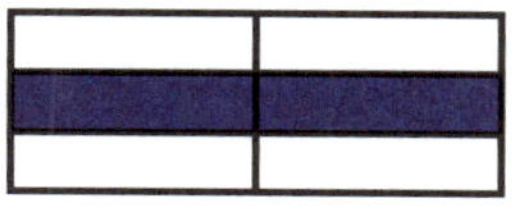 ___

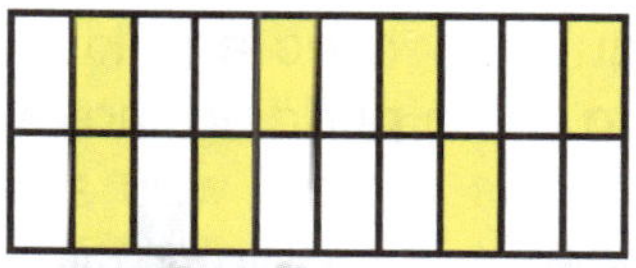 ___

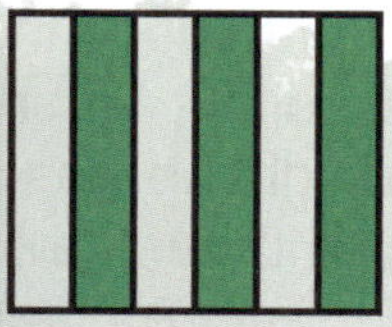 ___

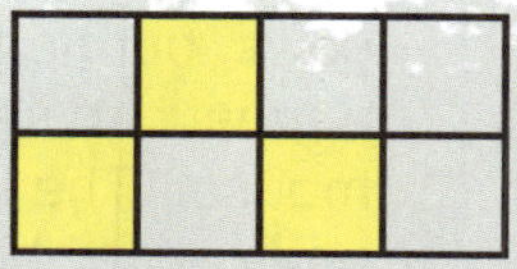 ___

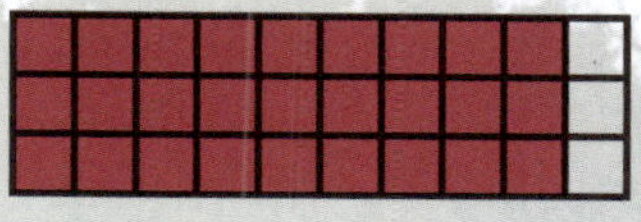 ___

Put periods in the paragraph where they belong.

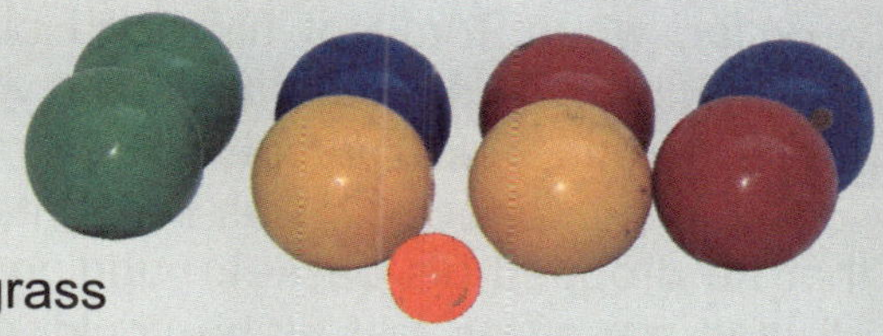

Bocce ball is a fun game to play The small ball, called the jack, is thrown out into the grass Then each team takes a turn throwing a ball The teams try to get their balls closest to the jack The teams keep taking turns until all the balls have been thrown Points are scored by the team with their balls closest to the jack

Underline each adjective and draw an arrow to the word it describes.

1. That new coat and long scarf do not match at all.
2. The busy ant hurried away to his anthill with a large crumb of bread.
3. Why is that small box on the table in the kitchen?
4. It is nice to see the green grass, blue sky and pretty flowers on a sunny day.
5. Red roses and white carnations make a lovely bouquet.

Tom Thumb
An English Fairy Tale

Tom never grew any larger than a man's thumb, so many interesting things happened to him. One day his mother was mixing a pudding. Tom leaned over the edge of the bowl to see how it was made. He slipped, and in he went, head first. His mother did not see him fall and kept stirring the pudding. Tom could not see nor hear, but he kicked and kicked inside the pudding. The pudding moved and tossed about. His mother was afraid. She did not know what to think. "Something must be wrong with it," she said.

She went to the window to throw the pudding out. Just then a poor beggar was passing by the house. "Here is a pudding you may have, if you like," said Tom's mother. The beggar thanked her and put it into his basket. He had not gone very far, when Tom got his head out of the pudding and shouted in a shrill voice: "Take me out! Take me out!"

The poor beggar was so frightened that he dropped his basket, pudding and all, and ran off as fast as he could. Tom crawled out of the pudding, climbed out of the basket, and ran home. His mother washed him and put him to bed.

Not long afterward, his mother took him with her when she went to milk the cow. She tied him to a wisp of hay so that he would not get lost. When Tom's mother was not looking, the cow took the wisp of hay into her mouth. She began to chew and chew. Tom began to jump about and shout. He frightened the cow so that she opened her great mouth and out Tom jumped. Then Tom's mother took him in her apron and ran with him to the house. He was not hurt in the least.

One time Tom was in the field helping his father. "May I drive the horse home?" asked Tom. "I could stand in the horse's ear and tell him which way to go," said Tom. So his father put him in the horse's ear, and he drove safely home. "Mother!" cried Tom, but when Tom's mother came out, she could not see him and began to be afraid. "Here I am in the horse's ear. Please take me down," said Tom.

His mother lifted him gently down, kissed him, and gave him a blackberry for his supper. Tom's father made him a whip out of a straw. Tom tried to drive the cows, but he fell into a deep ditch. There a great bird saw him and thought he was a mouse. The bird seized Tom in her claws and carried him toward her nest. As they were passing over the sea, Tom got away and fell into the water, where a great fish swallowed him.

When the fish was caught, it was so big that it was sent to the king. When the cook cut open the fish, out jumped Tom Thumb. Tom was brought before the king and told his story.

The king grew very fond of Tom. He took Tom with him wherever he went. If it began to rain, Tom would creep into the king's pocket and sleep until the rain was over. The king had a new suit made for Tom and gave him a needle for a sword. A mouse was trained for Tom to ride.

One day, as they were going hunting, a cat jumped out and caught Tom's mouse. Tom drew his sword and tried to drive the cat away. The king ran to help poor Tom, but the little mouse was dead, and Tom was scratched and bitten. Tom was put to bed, but he did not die. No indeed! He was soon well again and fought many brave battles and did many brave deeds to please the king.

On a separate sheet of paper, write about another adventure that could have happened to Tom.

Wednesday

Subtract.

933	727	928	545	841	602	820	661
- 496	- 382	- 190	- 498	- 257	- 91	- 354	- 229

Put **<** *or* **>** *in the circle.*

56 ÷ 8 ◯ 40 ÷ 5	17 - 9 ◯ 35 ÷ 7	48 ÷ 8 ◯ 11 - 6	18 - 9 ◯ 14 - 6
63 ÷ 7 ◯ 54 ÷ 9	12 - 5 ◯ 56 ÷ 7	42 ÷ 6 ◯ 11 - 5	13 - 7 ◯ 16 - 8
64 ÷ 8 ◯ 54 ÷ 6	13 - 8 ◯ 63 ÷ 9	30 ÷ 5 ◯ 16 - 7	14 - 5 ◯ 16 - 9

Write ***us***, ***you***, *or* ***them*** *on the line.*

1. It was very nice of _____________ to share their sand toys with _____________.
2. Have _____________ ever ridden a little boat like this at the sea shore?
3. The rain got _____________ all wet because we didn't have an umbrella.
4. Be careful when _____________ are out in those waves!
5. Kelly, did ___________ thank _____________ for sharing their things with us?

Place commas where they belong.

1. Buffalo NY is about one hundred miles from Erie PA.
2. Mr. Little likes ham cheese onions and green peppers in his omelette.
3. Do you know who was born on April 2 1968?
4. Gerbils hamsters mice and rats are all rodents.
5. Joshua's uncle was rescued on February 27 1977.

☆ **Something Extra**

Can you say the alphabet backwards? Give someone this page so they can see if you get it right.

z y x w v u t s r q p o n m l k j i h g f e d c b a

Finish the graph. Use separate lines for the high temperatures and the low temperatures.

	Sun.	Mon.	Tues.	Wed.	Thurs.	Fri.	Sat.
High	75	80	83	82	82	79	81
Low	69	71	70	70	68	69	69

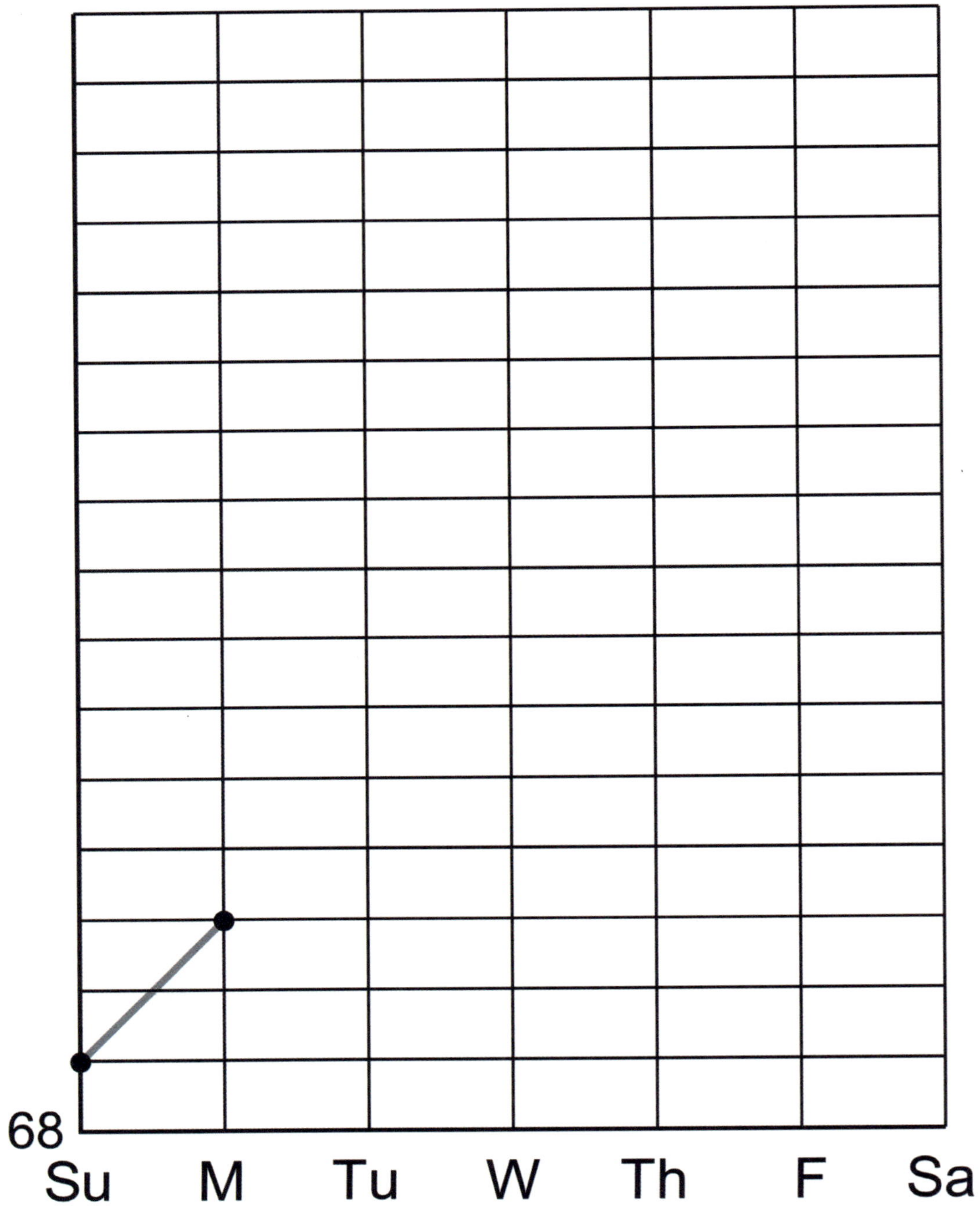

Thursday

Divide.

64 ÷ 8 = _____   25 ÷ 5 = _____   9 ÷ 3 = _____   12 ÷ 4 = _____

14 ÷ 2 = _____   18 ÷ 2 = _____   1 ÷ 1 = _____   36 ÷ 9 = _____

36 ÷ 4 = _____   48 ÷ 8 = _____   0 ÷ 5 = _____   21 ÷ 7 = _____

Add.

94	87	479	23	298	273	182	96
18	535	64	41	143	485	55	414
+ 59	+ 62	+ 76	+ 346	+ 517	+ 31	+ 348	+ 557

Choose three of the phrases below and use each of them in a complete sentence.

splashing each other   a shaggy dog   running as fast as he could

a tiny, little mouse   a long flowing streamer

____

____

____

Make the dark word plural and write it on the lines to make a good sentence.

penny 1. Jan has saved three quarters and six ________________.

foot 2. Do you know how many ________________ a caterpillar has?

half 3. James very carefully cut the candy bars into ________________.

woman 4. The ________________ in the choir all sang beautifully.

loaf 5. Mother baked five ________________ of bread yesterday.

Number each group of words in alphabetical order.

_____ Saturday	_____ size	_____ shell	_____ skate
_____ selfish	_____ sack	_____ slurp	_____ sardine
_____ share	_____ shiver	_____ side	_____ scope
_____ scrap	_____ skill	_____ saw	_____ seat
_____ seven	_____ seal	_____ second	_____ slim

Place a check mark in the correct box.

Word	Guide Words	Relation to the Page		
1. wise	wisdom - wonder	☐ before	☑ on	☐ after
2. ransom	redeem - review	☐ before	☐ on	☐ after
3. mouth	Michigan - missed	☐ before	☐ on	☐ after
4. bow	beau - breeze	☐ before	☐ on	☐ after
5. exalt	esteem - everlasting	☐ before	☐ on	☐ after
6. sword	skill - sorry	☐ before	☐ on	☐ after
7. prudent	patient - peculiar	☐ before	☐ on	☐ after
8. kind	keep - kitchen	☐ before	☐ on	☐ after
9. gate	genteel - gentle	☐ before	☐ on	☐ after
10. truth	tea - tulip	☐ before	☐ on	☐ after
11. ox	obey - peculiar	☐ before	☐ on	☐ after
12. understand	umbrella - violin	☐ before	☐ on	☐ after

Write the numeral for these number words.

four thousand, three hundred sixty-five ______________________

eight hundred thirteen thousand, nine hundred two ______________________

sixty thousand, four hundred seventy ______________________

seven million, twelve thousand, three ______________________

Solve these story problems.

1. Mr. King has 31 children in his 4th grade class. 17 of them are boys, and 14 are girls. If 4 children were absent yesterday, how many were at school?

____

2. Morgan took the bus downtown for $0.75. Then he got on another bus to go to the park for a game of Frisbee with his friends. That cost $0.35. How much will it cost him to go to the park and get back home?

____

3. Bill is saving for a new Ultra-Frisbee which costs $16. He earns $5.50 a week mowing lawns. How many weeks will it take him to earn enough to buy the Ultra-Frisbee?

____

*Tell whether the pairs of words are synonyms (**syn.**), antonyms (**ant.**) or homonyms (**hom.**).*

boy, girl ____________	car, automobile ________	rain, reign ____________
sign, banner __________	to, two ______________	heavy, light __________
slay, sleigh __________	young, old ____________	small, little __________
truth, lie ____________	pop, soda ____________	scene, seen __________

Write a letter to a relative whom you haven't seen recently. Tell them about what you have been doing this summer. Check your letter by the questions below. Then have an adult help you address the envelope and mail it.

_____ Did you write neatly?

_____ Did you use capital letters and periods?

_____ Are all the words spelled correctly?

The Marmot
from *An Alphabet of Quadrupeds*

Marmots live in the Alps and other high mountains. They live right below the area that always has snow. They are about the size of a hare and are a yellowish green color. Marmots live in families. They work together to build the home. The room in which they live is lined with dried grass and is at the end of a passage. The passage is six or eight feet long and forms the letter *Y*. One of the branches is the entrance. The other is a sewer. During winter, the mouth of the passage is closed by earth. Marmots eat together, but they always have a guard. At the first sign of danger, the guard utters a shrill cry and the whole group leaves.

Answer the questions about the paragraph.

1. What is a sewer?____________________________________

2. What do marmots always have when they are eating?________________

3. Marmots live on what kind of land? mountain valley plain

4. Marmots are most like the size of what animals? ants raccoons tigers

5. Draw a picture of the marmots' home based on the description in the paragraph.

Answer Key

Sometimes there will be more than one right answer to a question. Only one answer is listed in the answer key, but any correct answer should be accepted.

When a child is asked to wrtie, check to see that the child used proper spelling and punctuation. A child should always use his or her best handwriting.

front

Monday

Add.

71	54	30	25	99	76	42	92	78	33
+ 49	+ 97	+ 68	+ 83	+ 12	+ 28	+ 46	+ 39	+ 4	+ 91
120	151	98	108	111	104	88	131	82	124

Subtract to find how much change should be made. Draw coins to show the change.

Randy bought a race car for $4.79. He paid $5.00. $0.21 10¢ 10¢ 1¢

Susan bought a necklace for $3.14. She paid $3.50. $0.36 25¢ 10¢ 1¢

Hannah bought a dozen eggs for $0.67. She paid $1.00. $0.33 25¢ 5¢ 1¢ 1¢ 1¢

Joe bought a candy bar for $0.39. He paid $0.50. $0.11 10¢ 1¢

Put a ✓ over the underlined word if it is a noun. Put an X over the word if it is not a noun.

1. My grandfather and I like to fish from the small dock in his backyard.
2. We often go fishing very early in the morning before the sun gets too hot.
3. Sometimes I accidentally catch a turtle instead of a catfish or a bass.
4. Grandfather helps me put the bait on the hook and take the fish off the hook

Circle the letters in the story that should be a capital letter.

last july, i went to the mountains for a camping trip. i left on friday afternoon. on saturday, july 4th, i decided to take an extra long hike because it was independence day. i hiked and hiked for several hours. when i got back to my campsite, my friend julie was there. i was surprised to see her. after we ate supper, we roasted marshmallows over the fire. it was a wonderful 4th of july.

1

page 1

back

Number each group of items in order from least to greatest.

7 year, 1 second, 5 week, 2 minute, 6 month, 3 hour, 4 day

2 inch, 1 centimeter, 4 yard, 3 foot, 5 meter, 6 mile

6 senior citizen, 1 infant, 5 adult, 3 child, 4 teenager, 2 toddler

2 larva, 1 egg, 4 adult, 3 pupa

3 city, 4 state, 1 house, 2 street, 5 country

2 floor, 4 roof, 1 foundation, 3 walls

2 flour, 3 dough, 1 wheat, 4 bread, 5 sandwich

2 sauce, 1 crust, 4 toppings, 3 cheese, 5 eating

1 ice cream, 3 whipped topping, 4 cherry, 2 fudge sauce

front

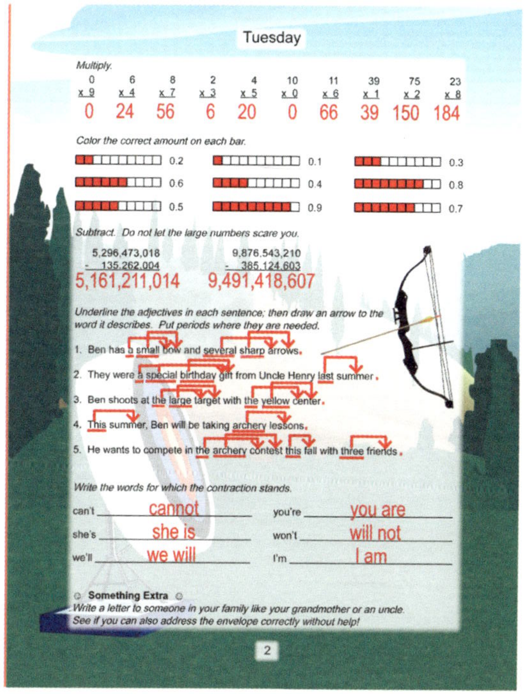

Tuesday

Multiply.

0	6	8	2	4	10	11	39	75	23
x 9	x 4	x 7	x 3	x 5	x 0	x 6	x 1	x 2	x 8
0	24	56	6	20	0	66	39	150	184

Color the correct amount on each bar.

0.2 0.1 0.3 0.6 0.4 0.8 0.5 0.9 0.7

Subtract. Do not let the large numbers scare you.

5,296,473,018 − 135,262,004 = 5,161,211,014

9,876,543,210 − 385,124,603 = 9,491,418,607

Underline the adjectives in each sentence; then draw an arrow to the word it describes. Put periods where they are needed.

1. Ben has a small bow and several sharp arrows.
2. They were a special birthday gift from Uncle Henry last summer.
3. Ben shoots at the large target with the yellow center.
4. This summer, Ben will be taking archery lessons.
5. He wants to compete in the archery contest this fall with three friends.

Write the words for which the contraction stands.

can't cannot — you're you are

she's she is — won't will not

we'll we will — I'm I am

Something Extra

Write a letter to someone in your family like your grandmother or an uncle. See if you can also address the envelope correctly without help!

2

page 2

back

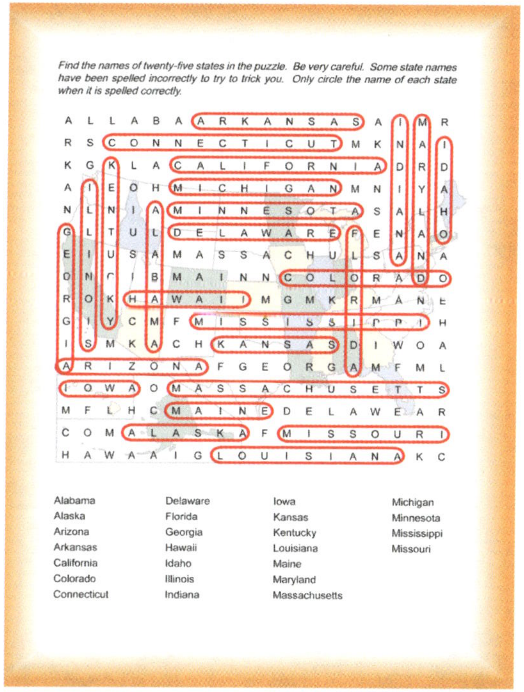

Find the names of twenty-five states in the puzzle. Be very careful. Some state names have been spelled incorrectly to try to trick you. Only circle the name of each state when it is spelled correctly.

A L L A B A A R K A N S A S A I M R
R S C O N N E C T I C U T M K N A I
K G K L A C A L I F O R N I A D R D
A I E O H M I C H I G A N M N I Y A
N L N I A M I N N E S O T A S A L H
G L T U L D E L A W A R E F E N A O
E I U S A M A S S A C H U L S A N A
O N C I B M A I N N C O L O R A D O
R O K H A W A I I M G M K R M A N E
G I Y C M F M I S S I S S I P P I H
I S M K A C H K A N S A S D I W O A
A R I Z O N A F G E O R G A M F M L
I O W A O M A S S A C H U S E T T S
M F L H C M A I N E D E L A W E A R
C O M A L A S K A F M I S S O U R I
H A W A A I G L O U I S I A N A K C

Alabama, Alaska, Arizona, Arkansas, California, Colorado, Connecticut, Delaware, Florida, Georgia, Hawaii, Idaho, Illinois, Indiana, Iowa, Kansas, Kentucky, Louisiana, Maine, Maryland, Massachusetts, Michigan, Minnesota, Mississippi, Missouri

front

page 3

Wednesday

Subtract.

511	832	673	940	724	862	570	793
- 409	- 197	- 85	- 368	- 256	- 337	- 108	- 59
102	635	588	572	468	525	462	734

Use the numbers to make four equations.

3 21 7

3 x 7 = 21
7 x 3 = 21
21 ÷ 3 = 7
21 ÷ 7 = 3

2 18 9

2 x 9 = 18
9 x 2 = 18
18 ÷ 2 = 9
18 ÷ 9 = 2

5 10 2

2 x 5 = 10
5 x 2 = 10
10 ÷ 2 = 5
10 ÷ 5 = 2

Put the correct punctuation at the end of each sentence. Then tell whether the sentence is **exclamatory**, **declarative** *or* **interrogative**.

declarative 1. The boys on Covington Drive like to play street hockey.
interrogative 2. Do you know when the next game will be?
declarative 3. The boys usually play on George's large, long driveway.
exclamatory 4. Yeah! Peter scored a goal!
interrogative 5. Have you ever played street hockey?

Place commas in the sentences.

1. Yes, Kendra, you may go to the party.
2. The President lives in Washington, D. C.
3. No, Mr. Hankins is not in his office right now.
4. John, would you, please, close the door?
5. Thomas Edison's research laboratory was built in Menlo Park, New Jersey.

Try This!
Take an empty plastic milk jug and rinse it with HOT water until the jug is hot all over. Now pour out the water and put the cap on tightly. Set it in the freezer and wait 20 minutes. Can you explain what happened?

3

front

page 4

Thursday

Divide.

16 ÷ 8 = 2 20 ÷ 4 = 5 2 ÷ 1 = 2 42 ÷ 6 = 7
9 ÷ 3 = 3 16 ÷ 2 = 8 28 ÷ 7 = 4 0 ÷ 5 = 0
54 ÷ 9 = 6 2 ÷ 2 = 1 45 ÷ 9 = 5 12 ÷ 2 = 6

Add.

34	391	89	95	177	53	11	425
72	247	65	42	121	84	45	274
+ 58	+ 423	+ 16	+ 28	+ 536	+ 69	+ 97	+ 351
164	1,061	170	165	834	206	153	1,050

Write the plural form of the words on the lines.

city cities glass glasses tree trees
bench benches daddy daddies leaf leaves
cat cats church churches copy copies
knife knives ball balls class classes

Number the words in each column in alphabetical order.

1 bear	3 Joseph	3 Rachel	3 maple
5 lion	4 Nathan	4 Sarah	4 oak
2 bird	2 James	1 Alice	5 pine
3 frog	5 Peter	5 Susan	2 aspen
4 lamb	1 Doug	2 Angela	1 apple

Circle the correct word.

1. Don't eat (to, two, too) much candy before the game or you will feel sick.
2. I am going (to, two, too) learn (to, two, too) juggle more than (to, too, two) clubs.
3. Juggling is not (to, too, two) hard if a person will practice a lot.
4. At the circus, (to, too, two) men juggled clubs (together, toogether).

4

front

page 5

Friday

In what place is the seven?

75 tens 4726 hundreds 7 ones
607 ones 5397 ones 67,253 thousands
7426 thousands 79 tens 979 tens

Solve the story problems.

1. Alston Classical School has 215 in the elementary school and 117 in the high school. How many students do they have altogether?
215 + 117 = 332

2. Mrs. Burns makes aprons. She can make two aprons from one yard of material. If she has ten yards of blue material, how many aprons can she make?
10 x 2 = 20

3. Doug bought a race car for $2.37 and a dump truck for $2.69. If he gave the clerk $6.00, how much change should he receive?
$2.37 + $2.69 = $5.06 $6.00 - $5.06 = $0.94

4. Monica wanted to share her bag of 12 cookies fairly with her 3 friends. How many cookies should she give to each person? (Monica also plans to eat cookies.)
12 ÷ 4 = 3

Put the quotation marks where they belong in the paragraph.

"Jenna, do you want to play volleyball?" asked Teresa. "We bought a new net yesterday."

"Sure," said Jenna. "That sounds like fun. Let's ask Mary and Ginger to join us."

"I'll go ask Mary while you ask Ginger," offered Teresa. "I'll meet you in my backyard in a couple of minutes."

Underline the subject(s) once and the verb(s) twice.

1. The horses galloped and chased each other around the pasture.
2. It is warm and sunny outside today.
3. The car swerved around the sharp corner.
4. The lightning flashed and the thunder crashed.
5. The dictionary is a great big book.

5

back

Fill in each blank with the best word from the bottom of the page.

George Washington was a great man, not because he was our first President, but because he was an honest man and tried to do right every day.

He knew that it is better to think of others before we think about ourselves. When George Washington was young, he listed rules for good manners in a notebook and tried very carefully to live by them. He always treated others and did each job, great or small, to the best of his ability. Surveyor, planter, soldier, burgess, delegate or President, he worked diligently and did each job well.

At his death, the entire nation mourned. His character and testimony have been honored and respected for many years. In Washington D. C. the Washington National Monument was built in memory of his life and leadership. The state of Washington was named after President Washington and his picture is on the Washington state flag.

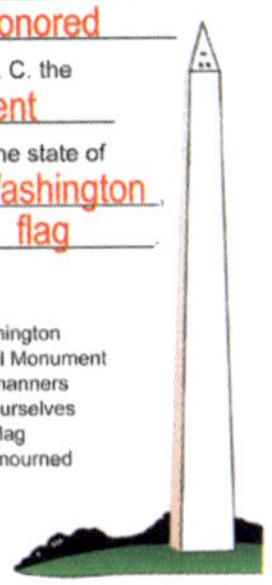

President Washington
Washington National Monument
honored manners
courteously ourselves
President flag
diligently mourned
right

back

Hint Hunter

Hint Hunter pages are a chance for you to use your brain to figure out something that you have never been told. Here is an example:

Heather, Helen, and Hannah each have a different pet. Heather keeps her pet in a glass bowl on her dresser. Hannah walks her pet every day. Circle the pet that belongs to each girl.

Now think about what you just read. Which would you keep in a glass bowl? A dog? No. A goldfish may be kept in a glass bowl. So Heather has a goldfish, and the other two girls do not. Circle Heather's goldfish and put an X on the other two fish. You can also put X's on the parakeet and the dog in Heather's row because she only has one pet.

Now, which pet would you take for a walk? A dog, so circle Hannah's dog and put an X on the other dogs. You can also put an X on the other pets in Hannah's row. Which pet is left for Helen? The parakeet.

When you are done, your paper should look like this.

Now you try this one.

Four boys went to the sporting goods store and bought something different. Carl plans to use what he bought when he is in the basement with his dad. Adam did not buy a ball. Bobby's purchase was round. What did each boy buy?

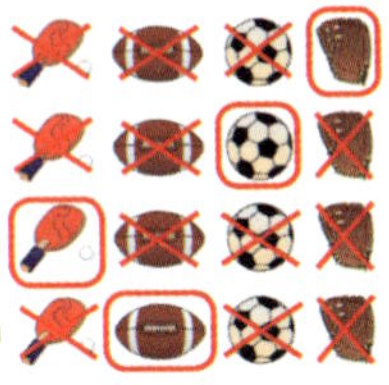

back

The Gnat and the Lion
Aesop

A gnat once went up to a lion and said, "I am not in the least afraid of you. I don't even think that you are a match for me in strength. What does your strength amount to after all? You can scratch with your claws and bite with your teeth and nothing more. But I am stronger than you. If you don't believe it, let us fight and see."

So saying, the gnat sounded his horn, and darted in and bit the lion on the nose. When the lion felt the sting, in his haste to crush him, he scratched his nose badly and made it bleed. But he did not hurt the gnat at all.

The gnat buzzed off in triumph, happy about his victory. Presently, however, he was caught in a spider's web and was eaten by the spider. Thus, he fell prey to an insignificant creature after having triumphed over the King of the Beasts.

Answer the questions about the story.

1. Which animal was bragging? (gnat) lion spider
2. Circle the antonym for *haste*. hurry (slow) hate
3. Write a homonym for *prey*. pray
4. What is the moral of this story?
People who go about bragging often suffer a real problem soon after they were bragging.

front

page 6

Monday

Add.

$2.84	$5.17	349	$1.37	$3.15	245	$5.68
+ .56	+ 1.75	+ 408	+ .66	+ .98	+ 424	+ .26
$3.40	$6.92	757	$2.03	$4.13	669	$5.94

Use the numbers to make four math facts.

7 9 2	8 12 4	6 10 4
2 + 7 = 9	4 + 8 = 12	4 + 6 = 10
7 + 2 = 9	8 + 4 = 12	6 + 4 = 10
9 - 2 = 7	12 - 4 = 8	10 - 4 = 6
9 - 7 = 2	12 - 8 = 4	10 - 6 = 4

In what place is the five?

524 hundreds 500,713 hundred thousands 98,650 tens

657,902 ten thousands 25,391 thousands 405 ones

Write a noun on each blank to make a good story. Answers will vary.

I have a pet named Toby. He is lots of fun. I like to play ball with him. His favorite toy is a stick. At night, he sleeps in my room. My pet has soft fur. He especially likes me to rub his ears. Don't you wish you had a pet like mine?

Circle the letters that should be capitalized.

1. (i) received a new unicycle for (c)hristmas.
2. (u)ncle (s)tephen tried to teach me to ride it.
3. (o)n (s)aturday (d)ad is going to try to help me again.
4. (i) am sure (i) will love it once (i) learn how to ride it.
5. (g)randpa and (g)randma will be here for (t)hanksgiving and (i) want to ride it well in front of them.

6

back

Choose the operation or operations you would need to do to find the answer. You do not have to solve the problems.

Belinda's Balloon Boutique

Bright balloon bunches–a bargain!

1. Belinda sells a dozen balloons for $17.40. How much is she charging per balloon?

   add subtract multiply (divide)

2. Belinda is having a special. When you buy two big balloons for $2.15 each, the third one is free. How much would six balloons cost during the special?

   add subtract (multiply) divide

3. Arnold's Accounting Service is giving a big retirement party to Mr. Tilgore who has worked there for over thirty years. They are decorating with four dozen balloons that cost $17.40 per dozen and one special retirement balloon that costs $4.75. How much are they going to spend on balloons?

   Step 1: add subtract (multiply) divide

   Step 2: (add) subtract multiply divide

4. Belinda usually keeps thirty-six balloons inflated to decorate the store. This morning when she arrived, she noticed she only had twenty-seven. How many more balloons does she need?

   add (subtract) multiply divide

5. Usually Belinda's store is very busy and she sells six hundred fifty balloons each week. Last week Belinda sold one thousand balloons. How many extra balloons did she sell last week?

   add (subtract) multiply divide

6. Henry bought one big balloon for $2.15 and a small balloon for $1.25. How much was his total?

   (add) subtract multiply divide

7. Three friends agreed to split the cost of the balloons for their other friend's surprise birthday party. They decided to get a dozen balloons for $17.40, a special birthday balloon for $3.50, and a balloon with a big ten on it for $2.80. How much did each girl have to pay?

   Step 1: (add) subtract multiply divide

   Step 2: add subtract multiply (divide)

Optional
For extra practice, go ahead and solve each problem.

front

page 7

Tuesday

Multiply.

7 x 10 = 70	1 x 1 = 1	7 x 3 = 21	2 x 5 = 10
9 x 9 = 81	5 x 7 = 35	10 x 4 = 40	8 x 6 = 48
6 x 0 = 0	4 x 8 = 32	0 x 2 = 0	3 x 10 = 30

Write the correct fraction.

$\frac{1}{3}$ $\frac{2}{5}$ $\frac{5}{12}$

$\frac{1}{2}$ $\frac{3}{5}$ $\frac{6}{12}$ $\frac{2}{3}$

Circle the adjectives in the sentences.

1. (My) mother grows (red) tulips, (yellow) daffodils and (purple) crocuses in (her) yard.
2. Dick found (a) (bright) (shiny) penny in (the) (wet) grass.
3. (The) (black) (hairy) spider crawled up (the) (brick) wall.
4. Derek enjoyed (the) (crispy) (crunchy) cookies.
5. He has (a) (yellow) marble, (a) (short) string and (a) (green) frog in (his) pockets.

Put periods where they belong in the story.

Last weekend Mr. T. J. Landing went camping on Mt. Misty. He invited his friend, James S. Thomas, to go with him. The two men set up camp. Then they hiked to old Ft. Lookout. When they got back, they fixed a big supper and went to bed. A few hours later the men heard strange noises. What do you think they saw when they looked out of the tent?

Circle the correct word.

1. The teacher (taught) learned) the class how to divide.
2. The boys (taught (learned) how to bait a hook.
3. Will you please (teach) learn) me how to build a fire?

7

back

A Quiet Talk with the Looking Glass
from *Childhood's Happy Hours*

If a mirror could speak, what strange things it would say. Some things we might not like to hear. It might say to Agnes, "Aggie, you are a good girl, but you spend too much time looking at me." Or to Robert, "Bob, there is no reason for you to go rushing around in such a hurry. You go to school without even looking at me. Your hair looks as if it had not been brushed for a week."

But suppose the looking glass could tell you its history. It might tell you about its birth and growth, its travel in other lands, the people it has met and the treatment it has received. What a strange story it would be!

Write a story as if you were a mirror and were telling someone your history.

Answers will vary.

front

page 8

Wednesday

Subtract.

$53.79	2460	2897	$42.18	9514	7256
- 4.86	- 501	- 613	- 3.70	- 803	- 931
$48.93	1,959	2,284	$38.48	8,711	6,325

Put < or > in the circle.

9 + 9 > 3 x 3	2 + 7 < 3 + 7	4 x 9 > 8 x 4	3 x 5 > 6 + 5
6 + 7 > 4 x 0	8 + 5 > 0 + 9	9 x 5 > 1 x 8	8 x 1 < 4 + 7
1 + 6 < 5 x 4	8 + 6 > 1 + 2	2 x 4 < 5 x 6	1 x 6 > 1 + 3

Fill in the temperatures.

18° 84° 40° 16° 28° 51°

Use **he, she,** *or* **it** *in the sentences.*

1. Benjamin thinks it is fun to slide down the slide.
2. Sarah is very little; she is afraid to go down the slide.
3. I think it is fun to slide with my eyes closed.
4. David tried to climb up the slide, but he could not.
5. Susan likes the slide, but she thinks the swings are the best.

Put commas where they belong.

1. Mother bought milk, eggs, bread and soup at the grocery store this morning.
2. On July 4, 1776, our country became a separate nation.
3. No, Bethany, you may not have six cookies for dessert.
4. The long, brown snake slithered quietly through the tall, green weeds.
5. George Washington was born on February 22, 1732, in Westmoreland, Virginia.

?? Can They Guess ??
Use the back of this page to write a description of one of your friends, but do not use his or her name. After you are finished, read it to someone and see if they can figure out who it is.

8

back

Cross out the item in each row that does not belong. Then tell why the other items belong together.

Example: banana ~~broccoli~~ apple pear
Why? *The other items are all fruits.*

1. Steven Sam ~~Sandra~~ Saul Scott
   Why? Sandra is not a boy's name.
2. whale ~~shark~~ giraffe bear raccoon
   Why? A shark lays eggs; it is not a mammal.
3. monitor mouse ~~radio~~ keyboard speakers
   Why? All the rest are parts of a computer.
4. Army Navy Air Force Marines ~~soldier~~ Coast Guard
   Why? All the others are branches of the military.
5. ash elm fir ~~ivy~~ oak
   Why? Ivy is not a kind of tree.
6. hamburger ~~jello~~ meatloaf tacos barbecue
   Why? Jello is not a meat.
7. ~~table~~ chair sofa couch bench
   Why? We do not sit on a table.
8. cricket ant butterfly roach ~~spider~~
   Why? A spider is not an insect.
9. President Mayor Governor ~~Doctor~~ Senator
   Why? A doctor is not an elected official.
10. lamp flashlight candle fire ~~tent~~
    Why? A tent does not give light.

front

page 9

Thursday

Divide.

36 ÷ 6 = 6	27 ÷ 9 = 3	72 ÷ 8 = 9	0 ÷ 7 = 0	4 ÷ 1 = 4	32 ÷ 4 = 8
16 ÷ 4 = 4	18 ÷ 6 = 3	10 ÷ 5 = 2	40 ÷ 8 = 5	3 ÷ 3 = 1	21 ÷ 3 = 7

Fill in the blanks. Remember: 12 inches=1 foot, 3 feet=1 yard

24 inches = 2 feet   9 feet = 3 yards   6 feet = 2 yards
2 yards = 6 feet   36 inches = 3 feet   2 feet = 24 inches
3 feet = 36 inches   3 yards = 9 feet   36 inches = 1 yard

Write **yes** *on the line if the words make a complete sentence. Write* **no** *if they do not make a complete sentence.*

no 1. A very long kick in between the goal posts.
yes 2. The receiver caught the ball.
no 3. Dark blue jerseys and bright yellow pants.
no 4. The thick green grass and white lines of the field.
yes 5. The Tigers scored fourteen points in the first half.

Make the bold word plural and write it on the line to finish the sentence.

elf 1. Have you ever read the story about the shoe maker and the elves?
lady 2. Many ladies like to go shopping.
box 3. Mrs. Smith carefully packed everything in large boxes.
thief 4. The police caught the thieves who tried to rob the bank.
shoe 5. Sam, I think your black shoes would look good with that suit.

back

Circle the word that is misspelled and write it correctly on the line.

1. (whitch) where whenever whose — which
2. necklace bracelet earrings (jewlry) — jewelry
3. width (hieght) depth length — height
4. grocery laundry (libary) hardware — library
5. mistake (mispell) misbehave mischief — misspell
6. (principel) teacher librarian secretary — principal
7. twenty thirty (fourty) fifty — forty
8. about around (untill) later — until
9. unusual different strange (wierd) — weird
10. finish (finaly) completely done — finally
11. calves intestine stomach (tounge) — tongue
12. (becuse) through also though — because

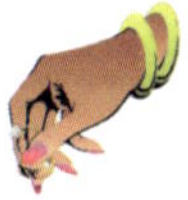

front

page 10

Friday

Fill in the missing numbers.

6 + 5 = 11   6 x 8 = 48   9 + 7 = 16   7 x 5 = 35
5 + 9 = 14   8 x 8 = 64   5 + 7 = 12   5 x 6 = 30
7 + 7 = 14   9 x 9 = 81   8 + 6 = 14   9 x 6 = 54

Solve these story problems.

1. Julie and Jan are saving money to buy a present for their dad. Together they have saved $3.75. They need $9.50. How much more do they need?
$9.50 - $3.75 = $5.75

2. Mr. Bates made 47 signs at work last week, and his partner made 28 signs. How many signs did they make altogether?
47 + 28 = 75

3. Grandpa's jalopy gets 12 miles per gallon. How far can he travel on 5 gallons of gas?
12 x 5 = 60

4. At Parker's part-time job he makes $7.00 on Tuesday and $9.00 on Thursday. How much does he make in 4 weeks?
$7.00 + $9.00 = $16.00 $16 x 4 = $64

Tell whether the pairs of words are synonyms **(syn.)**, *homonyms* **(hom.)** *or antonyms* **(ant.)**.

deer, dear hom.   up, down ant.   glad, happy syn.
hot, cold ant.   eight, ate hom.   large, big syn.
pear, pair hom.   near, close syn.   yes, no ant.
boy, lad syn.   stop, go ant.   meet, meat hom.

Circle the correct word.

1. (They're, Their, There) letting us stay with them at the beach.
2. Will you please spread out the towels over (they're, their, there)?
3. I love to play at the beach when (its, it's) sunny.
4. Did Susan help mother (set, sit) out the picnic lunch?
5. The wind (blew, blue) the water into big waves.

back

At West Point
from *Our Hero General U.S. Grant*

It was in the year 1839 that Grant went to West Point. West Point is a school where the drill is the same year in and year out. Young men are sent there from all parts of the United States to learn the art of war.

Ulysses did not need to be taught how to mount or to ride a horse. He knew all that. He made friends there who were good friends until the day of his death. These friends knew that he tried to do what was right, just and true and had a clear head and a pure mind.

He did not talk much, but he was as fond of fun as most boys are. It had to be the right kind of fun or he would not take part in it. He did not swear. He did not want to hear bad jokes, which is more than can be said of most men.

This one thing shows how brave Grant was at this time. He was firm to stick to what he thought was the right course. He had set out to be a good man and a clean man. God gave him strength to turn from all that was bad and to live so that he would not have to blush with shame for his past deeds. He could not have known then how high he was to stand in the eyes of the world. He did not know how each act of his life would be brought and held up to view in the clear light of fame.

Answer the questions about General Grant.

1. What is West Point? (a school) a battle a man
2. Using two or three complete sentences, describe General Grant's character while he was at West Point.
He was honest and tried to do right all the time.
He had a clear head and a pure mind.

front

page 11

Monday

Add.

395	269	405	156	370	543	484	502
+ 532	+ 152	+ 211	+ 63	+ 426	+ 120	+ 250	+ 440
927	421	616	219	796	663	734	942

Subtract to find how much change should be made. Draw coins to show the change.

Mrs. Neal bought a tomato plant for $2.43. She paid $3.00. $0.57 (25¢) (25¢) (5¢) (1¢) (1¢)	Mr. Bill bought a shovel for $5.82. He paid $6.00. $0.18 (10¢) (5¢) (1¢) (1¢) (1¢)
Mr. Lucas bought some fertilizer for $9.22. He paid $9.25. $0.03 (1¢) (1¢) (1¢)	Miss Spring bought some tulips for $3.17. She paid $3.25. $0.08 (5¢) (1¢) (1¢) (1¢)

Put capital letters where they belong. Cross out any that do not belong.

Have you ever Read one morning in maine? it is a Cute story about a little girl named sal who lost her Tooth. the Tooth not only fell out of her mouth but also got lost before she could Put it under her pillow. sal tried To wish on a feather to see if she could still get her wish. you should read the Book to see what happened.

Circle all the nouns in the following sentences.

1. (Sarah) has a pogo (stick) that she shares with (Francis).
2. The (girls) like to hop down the (driveway) like a (kangaroo).
3. (Sarah) fell off quite a (bit) but she continued to practice.
4. Occasionally the (girls) have a bouncing (contest) to see who can hop the most (times).
5. (Sarah) also shares the pogo (stick) with her (brother) and his (friends).

back

Answer the questions about the map.

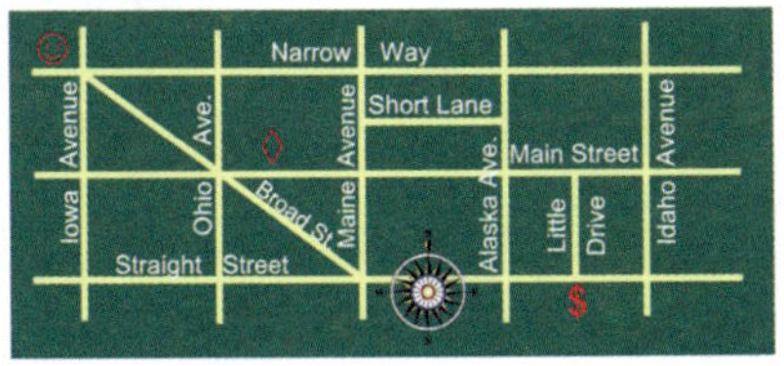

1. Ohio Avenue is between what other two Avenues? Iowa Avenue   Maine Avenue
2. The north end of Little Drive meets what street? Main Street
3. The south end of Broad Street touches the corner of what two streets? Straight Street   Maine Avenue
4. Which end of Short Lane is closest to Idaho Avenue? the east end
5. What street is south of Main Street? Straight Street
6. How many roads does Ohio Avenue cross? three
7. The town bank is at the south end of Little Drive. Put a $ at the bank's location.
8. The Vernons live on the north side of Main Street between Maine Avenue and Ohio Avenue. Put a ◊ where their house would be.
9. The new playground is being built on the west end of Narrow Way on the north side of the street. Put a ○ where the new playground is being built.

front

Tuesday

Multiply.

3 x 0	0 x 5	6 x 6	1 x 8	7 x 9	10 x 10	28 x 4	44 x 2	69 x 3	85 x 1
0	0	36	8	63	100	112	88	207	85

Draw and color the correct number of objects.

$2\frac{1}{3}$ $1\frac{3}{4}$ $3\frac{5}{6}$

Write adjectives on the lines to make a good story. Put periods where they are needed.

The Kingstons have a large garden. They grow sweet corn, yellow tomatoes and baby carrots. The gray squirrels and tiny bugs like the garden, too. Both Mr. and Mrs. Kingston work very hard in their vegetable garden on the farm.

Circle the correct word.

1. Jack (sit, set) the new bridle down very carefully.
2. Horses like to (lie, lay) on a soft bed of hay in a comfortable barn.
3. Please (sit, set) up straight in the saddle.
4. It is nice to be able to (lie, lay) down and take a nap when you're tired.
5. Mother (sit, set) the vase of flowers on the table.
6. Linda (sitted, sat) down slowly next to the nervous filly.

Something Special
Do an extra chore or favor for your mom or dad today, just to see them smile. It will probably make you smile, too.

12

page 12

back

Answer the questions about the portion of the dictionary page shown here.

performance - period

per·form·ance (pər-fôrməns) n. 1. The act of performing. 2. The way in which someone or something functions. 3. A presentation before an audience.
per·fume (pûr-fūm) n. 1. A liquid distilled from flowers that gives off a fragrant odor. 2. A pleasing, agreeable scent or odor. --v. To fill with fragrance; give a pleasing odor to.
per·fum·er (pûr-fūm- ər) n. A maker or seller of perfume.
per·haps (pər-hăps) adv. Maybe; possibly.
per·i·dot (pěr-ĭ-dōt) n. A green variety of olivine used as a gem.
per·il (pěr-əl) n. 1. A condition of imminent danger. 2. Something that endangers; serious risk.
pe·rim·e·ter (pə-rĭm-ĭ-tər) n. 1. a. *Math.* A closed curve bounding a plane area. b. The length of such a boundary. 2. The outer limits of an area.

1. Which of the following words would also be on this page?
   (perilous) punt pillow party
   pardon (perfusion) panda (pergola)
2. Which word on the page above can be used as a noun or a verb? perfume
3. Which word is used in math? perimeter
4. Which word might be the name of your birth stone? peridot
5. "The performance of the car was better than expected." Which definition is used in this sentence? 1 (2) 3
6. Use the word *perimeter* in a sentence and tell which definition you are using.
   A fence was put around the perimeter of the playground. - definition #2

front

Wednesday

Subtract and check by adding.

77 - 8	69 + 8	84 - 42	42 + 42	65 - 19	46 + 19	71 - 26	45 + 26
69	77	42	84	46	65	45	71

Use the numbers to make four equations.

4 28 7
4 x 7 = 28
7 x 4 = 28
28 ÷ 4 = 7
28 ÷ 7 = 4

8 40 5
5 x 8 = 40
8 x 5 = 40
40 ÷ 5 = 8
40 ÷ 8 = 5

6 1 6
1 x 6 = 6
6 x 1 = 6
6 ÷ 1 = 6
6 ÷ 6 = 1

Solve the story problem.

1. The town's water tower sprang a leak. It was nine minutes before the workers could get the leak stopped. If fifty gallons leaked out each minute, how much water was lost?
   50 x 9 = 450

Place commas in the sentences where they belong.

1. Mr. Stevens, there is a message for you on your answering machine.
2. The Jacksons raise goats, pigs, horses and chickens on their farm.
3. The Framptons visited Orlando, Florida on their vacation.
4. I am sorry, Mrs. Hollings, but we have run out of size five.
5. Robins, cardinals, crows and ravens are all types of birds.

Place the correct punctuation at the end of each sentence. Then tell whether the sentence is **exclamatory, declarative** *or* **interrogative**.

declarative 1. It is fun to watch the sea gulls at the seashore.
exclamatory 2. Look at the big claws on that crab!
interrogative 3. Did you bring the shovels and the buckets?
interrogative 4. What time will the next high tide occur?
declarative 5. I think we should build a great big sand castle.

13

page 13

back

Write the homonyms in the crossword puzzle.

Across
3. dough
5. fare
6. blew
8. capital
9. bye
10. ad
12. heir
13. fined
14. coarse
15. be
17. creak
18. (lemon) ade
19. cent

Down
1. bawl
2. hare
3. die
4. I
5. ferry
6. bored
7. bolder
9. break
10. ant
11. flour
13. flu
16. sell
17. sealing

front

Thursday

Divide.

$6\overline{)27}$ = 4 r3 $3\overline{)19}$ = 6 r1 $9\overline{)50}$ = 5 r5 $7\overline{)30}$ = 4 r2 $5\overline{)7}$ = 1 r2 $4\overline{)35}$ = 8 r3

$8\overline{)20}$ = 3 r2 $2\overline{)9}$ = 4 r1 $10\overline{)31}$ = 3 r1 $3\overline{)22}$ = 7 r1 $6\overline{)14}$ = 2 r2 $2\overline{)21}$ = 10 r1

Look at the graph and answer the questions.

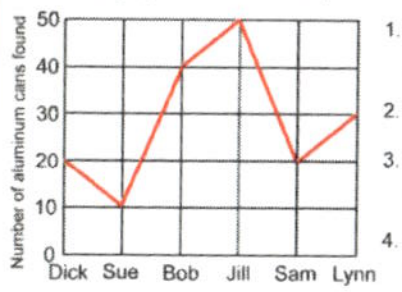

1. Who found more cans, Dick or Lynn? Lynn
2. Who found the most cans? Jill
3. Which two people found the same number of cans? Dick, Sam
4. Who found the most cans, the girls or the boys? girls

Use the dictionary to find out which words are spelled correctly. Circle the words that are spelled correctly.

(elephant) elephent   (Pennsylvania) Pensylvania   (squirrel) squirel
practise (practice)   sentance (sentence)   (giraffe) girrafe

Write the plural form of each word on the line.

sheaf sheaves   goose geese   bunch bunches
fly flies   mouse mice   fox foxes
wolf wolves   fish fish   rug rugs
guppy guppies   deer deer

Try This!
Get two small balls and see if you can learn to juggle them with one hand.

14

page 14

back

Starting with the word you are given, change one letter each time to make a new word.

meat

1.	to hit something a lot	b e a t
2.	a small, round ball used in a necklace or bracelet	b e a d
3.	to form a curve with force or pressure	b e n d
4.	to let someone borrow, especially money	l e n d
5.	ground; opposite of sea	l a n d
6.	road or small street	l a n e
7.	the shaggy hair on a male lion	m a n e
8.	opposite of female	m a l e
9.	5,280 feet	m i l e
10.	pleasant; far from extreme	m i l d
11.	the stuff that grows on old bread	m o l d
12.	a state of feeling, such as happy or sad	m o o d
13.	what shines at night	m o o n
14.	a groan, often from pain	m o a n
15.	not nice; rude or ugly in behavior	m e a n
16.	chicken, beef, or fish	m e a t

front

page 15

Friday

Tell whether the number is odd or even.

461 odd	8 even	99 odd	6392 even
32 even	63 odd	474 even	740 even
7864 even	935 odd	9761 odd	1 odd

Solve the story problems.

1. Valerie saw 6 birds, 4 butterflies, 27 ants, 5 crickets and 2 deer in the woods near her house. How many insects did she see?
   4 + 27 + 5 = 36
2. Mr. Andersen made $40 for working 8 hours last Thursday. How much did he make an hour?
   $40 ÷ 8 = 5
3. If Janet earns $162 a week, how much money does she earn in four weeks?
   $162 x 4 = $648
4. Mr. and Mrs. McCollum went on a 497 mile trip. They went 235 miles on the first day. How many more miles do they need to travel on the second day?
   497 - 235 = 262

Put quotation marks where they belong.

"Can you come over to my house?" asked Ned. "I would like to show you my new fish."

"I don't know," answered Peter. "I will have to ask my mom. Can you wait a minute?"

"Yes, I'll wait," said Ned. "Hurry up and ask her. I want to show the fish to you before lunch."

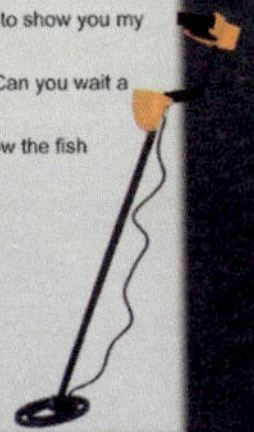

Underline each subject once and each verb twice.

1. My dad and I look for treasure together on weekends.
2. We use a metal detector, and we take a shovel with us.
3. Sometimes we find coins or locate old nails.
4. One Saturday I found a bracelet, and my dad found a knife.
5. Maybe one day we will find a really important treasure.

back

Sheep Shearing
from *McGuffey's Second Eclectic Reader*

Sheep are washed and sheared some time in the month of June. This should be done quite early in the month, before the hot days begin.

It is fun for the people watching, but not much fun for the sheep. It is best for the sheep to have the wool taken off. Otherwise, they would be too hot in the summertime.

When the time comes for washing the sheep, they are driven to a pond or a little river. Then they are thrown into the water, one at a time. The men who are in the water catch them, and squeeze the wet wool with their hands to get the dirt out of it.

When the wool is thoroughly dried, the sheep are taken to the shearer. He cuts off the wool with a large pair of shears. It is then dyed, spun, and woven into cloth.

In a short time, before the cold winter comes, new wool grows out on the sheep. By spring time there is so much that it must be cut off again.

Answer the questions about what you read.

1. Why do sheep need to be sheared? The sheep would get too hot if the wool were not cut.
2. Why are the sheep thrown into a pond?
   to cool off — (to be washed) — to have fun swimming
3. Write a synonym for the word *shears*. scissors
4. What type of writing is this selection?
   a story — (information) — a poem — an advertisement
5. Find something in your house that is made with wool. What color is it? Answers will vary.

front

page 16

Monday

Add.

$2.87 + 0.96	106 + 354	428 + 48	$3.04 + 2.86	195 + 46	465 + 535	$1.79 + 3.77
$3.83	460	476	$5.90	241	1000	$5.56

Use the numbers to make four math facts.

9 14 5	3 11 8	8 15 7
5 + 9 = 14	3 + 8 = 11	7 + 8 = 15
9 + 5 = 14	8 + 3 = 11	8 + 7 = 15
14 - 5 = 9	11 - 3 = 8	15 - 7 = 8
14 - 9 = 5	11 - 8 = 3	15 - 8 = 7

Fill in the temperatures.

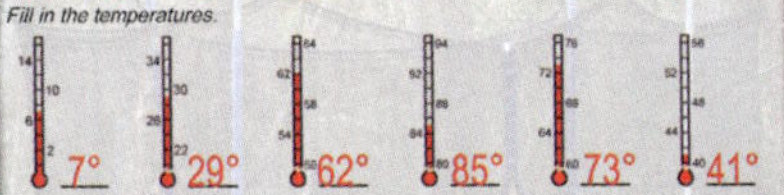

7° — 29° — 62° — 85° — 73° — 41°

Put a ✓ over the underlined word if it is a noun. Put an **X** *over the underlined word if it is not a noun.*

Dave (✓) and Holly have a trampoline in (X) their backyard (✓). They love to jump (X) on it and (X) do tricks. Dave usually (X) practices a front flip (✓) which is his favorite trick (✓). Holly, who takes gymnastics (✓), often works (X) on a jump called a Russian or (X) toe touch.

On most days (✓) Dave and (X) Holly have friends (✓) who come and jump with (X) them. But all the friends (✓) are very careful (X) to obey the safety rules (✓) so that they can (X) all have fun.

Put an X on the letters that should be capitalized and write the capital over them.

1. Valentine's Day comes on February 14th.
2. Mr. Smithers really enjoys collecting stamps from South America.
3. Do you know if the meeting will be on Wednesday or Thursday?
4. Our new home is at 275 Mountain View Parkway in Lacey Spring, Virginia.

back

Make a new word and write it on the line. There may be more than one word that can be made from the letters. Any good word is a fine answer.

Example: get + a = gate   goal - o = tag

1. super - s = pure, Peru
2. bus + s = subs
3. dairy - y = raid, arid
4. fat + s = fast, fats
5. heart - h = rate, tear, tare
6. grin + w = wring
7. page - e = gap
8. plead + e = leaped, pealed
9. weep - e = pew
10. barrel - r = blare

front

page 17

Tuesday

Multiply.

2 x 7 = 14	0 x 0 = 0	4 x 4 = 16	7 x 1 = 7
8 x 8 = 64	1 x 9 = 9	5 x 10 = 50	2 x 6 = 12
3 x 2 = 6	6 x 7 = 42	9 x 5 = 45	10 x 3 = 30

Write the correct fraction.

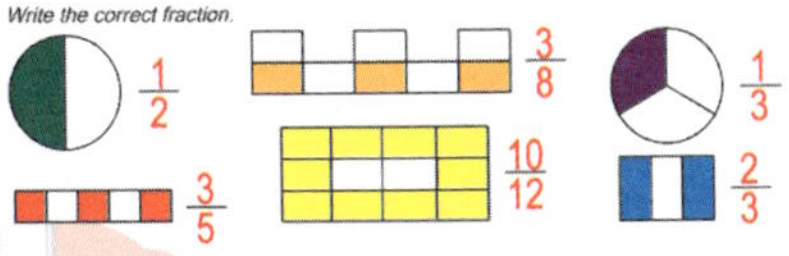

$\frac{1}{2}$ $\frac{3}{8}$ $\frac{1}{3}$ $\frac{3}{5}$ $\frac{10}{12}$ $\frac{2}{3}$

Put periods in the story where they belong.

Mr. B. L. Harrison is my neighbor. Mr. Harrison raises Dalmatians. His good friend, Dr. Cox, comes over at least once a week to check on Mr. Harrison's dogs. Both men love dogs. I am glad to have such an interesting neighbor right here on Hanover St.

Remember, adjectives are words that describe something. Underline the adjectives and draw an arrow to the word it describes.

1. Dr. Abrams, our local doctor, loves to play golf at the new golf course.
2. The new course has fresh green grass and bright flags.
3. Many of the men like to drive the shiny new golf carts.
4. The golf shop at the course sells many kinds of clubs and special clothes.

Just For Fun

Draw some faces or animals on balloons. Blow them up and watch what happens to your drawings.

back

It Isn't Costly
by Edgar A. Guest

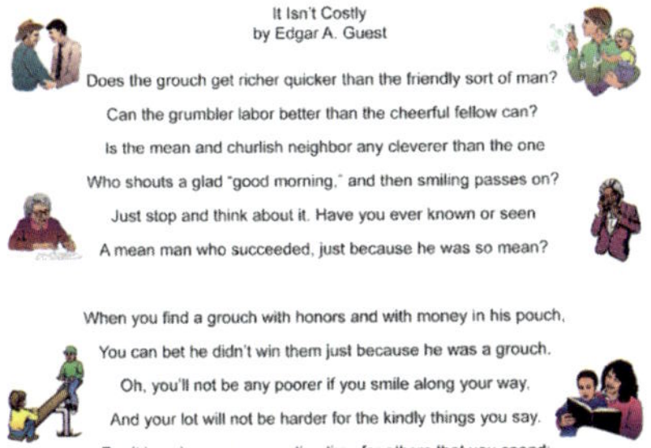

Does the grouch get richer quicker than the friendly sort of man?
Can the grumbler labor better than the cheerful fellow can?
Is the mean and churlish neighbor any cleverer than the one
Who shouts a glad "good morning," and then smiling passes on?
Just stop and think about it. Have you ever known or seen
A mean man who succeeded, just because he was so mean?

When you find a grouch with honors and with money in his pouch,
You can bet he didn't win them just because he was a grouch.
Oh, you'll not be any poorer if you smile along your way,
And your lot will not be harder for the kindly things you say.
Don't imagine you are wasting time for others that you spend:
You can rise to wealth and glory and still pause to be a friend.

Answer the questions about what you read.

1. What type of writing is this? (poem) — story — chapter
2. In one sentence write the main idea of this selection.
   It doesn't cost money to be nice and kind.
3. List three things that will not change in life just because you are grouchy.
   a. wealth
   b. work
   c. success
4. Who is the author of this selection? Edgar A. Guest

front

page 18

Wednesday

Subtract.

900	615	881	623	965	512	751	818
- 244	- 426	- 294	- 86	- 439	- 178	- 347	- 99
656	189	587	537	526	334	404	719

Put < or > in the circle.

10 - 5 < 42 ÷ 7	17 - 8 > 15 - 8	36 ÷ 6 < 72 ÷ 8	48 ÷ 6 > 12 - 6
13 - 6 < 72 ÷ 9	15 - 9 > 14 - 9	49 ÷ 7 > 25 ÷ 5	45 ÷ 9 < 13 - 5
15 - 6 > 40 ÷ 8	12 - 7 < 15 - 7	45 ÷ 5 > 35 ÷ 5	81 ÷ 9 > 14 - 8

What comes next?

2, 4, 6, 8, 10, 12, 14, 16, 18

4, 8, 12, 16, 20, 24, 28, 32, 36

6, 12, 18, 24, 30, 36, 42, 48, 54

Circle the correct word.

1. Brendan received a (knew, new) pair of stilts last week.
2. (Dew, Do) you know if he (asked, axed) for help with them?
3. Did anyone (sea, see) if he fell down a lot or (knot, not)?
4. Now Brendan can walk back and (forth, fourth) easily on his stilts.
5. Little Joe wants (to, too, two) try the stilts (himself, hisself).

Place commas where they belong in the paragraph.

On June 16, 2005, we moved from Greenville, North Carolina to Kewanee, Illinois. We were in our new house and unpacked by June 21, 2005. I liked our new home. It had three bedrooms, two bathrooms, a living room, a dining room and a kitchen. My brother Nathan liked the backyard the best. It had a few good climbing trees, a creek and lots of room for running around.

18

back

Finish labeling the graph and filling it in using the information you are given. Then answer the questions from your graph.

The neighborhood kids decided to set up an obstacle course and have a contest to see who could do it the fastest. They practiced all week and held the contest on Saturday. Their times were: Sandra - 6 min.; Benjamin - 4 min.; Nathan - 5 min.; Zena - 7 min.; Steve - 3 min.; Renee - 5 min.

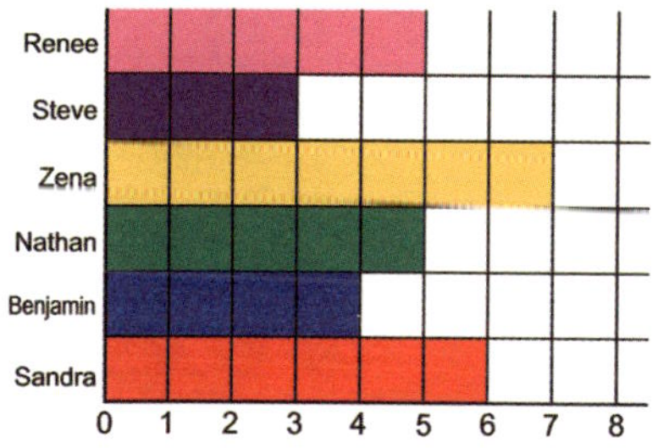

1. Who finished the obstacle course the fastest? Steve
2. Which two took the same amount of time? Renee and Nathan
3. How many minutes difference is there between the fastest and slowest times? four minutes
4. If the boys raced the girls as teams, which team do you think would win? Why? The boys because their total time was less.

front

page 19

Thursday

Divide.

81 ÷ 9 = 9	8 ÷ 2 = 4	27 ÷ 3 = 9	24 ÷ 4 = 6
24 ÷ 6 = 4	0 ÷ 1 = 0	36 ÷ 9 = 4	56 ÷ 7 = 8
15 ÷ 3 = 5	7 ÷ 1 = 7	42 ÷ 7 = 6	24 ÷ 8 = 3

Add.

83	239	99	86	563	332	281	43
566	48	14	378	193	61	526	54
+ 12	+ 37	+ 452	+ 117	+ 56	+ 449	+ 175	+ 67
661	324	565	581	812	842	982	164

Choose three of the incomplete sentences below and rewrite them to make complete sentences.

a gray goose — running away and yelling — the bright, red car — a red, white and blue flag — giggling and laughing

A gray goose wandered onto the tennis court.

Mr. Greg arrived in the bright red car.

The girls kept giggling and laughing when they missed the ball.

Write the plural form of each word on the line.

match matches	shelf shelves	child children
ox oxen	six sixes	chair chairs
life lives	man men	hand hands
bug bugs	wolf wolves	dress dresses

19

back

Hint Hunter

The Stokes children earned money doing extra chores during the week. Little Danny earned enough money to buy a small candy bar. Dianne earned the most and hoped she could buy a new pair of shoes. Duran wanted to use his money to get a hamburger and fries with his dad. Debbie wanted to buy a new necklace but does not have enough money. She put her money in her wallet and saved it. How much did each child earn?

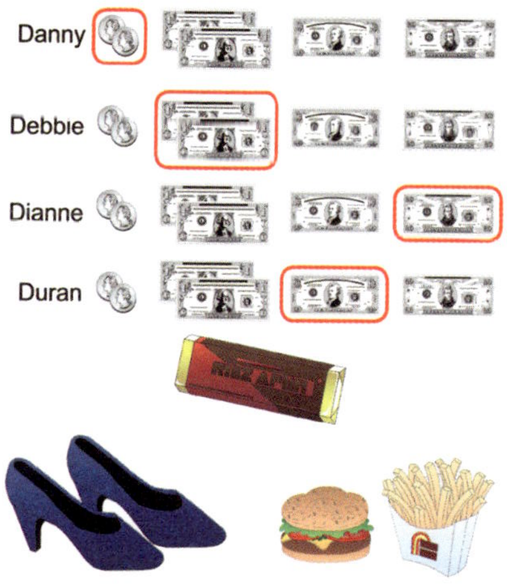

front

page 20

Friday

Solve these story problems.

1. Mrs. Parks has 28 apples, 6 of which are green. She divided them evenly among 4 of her neighbors. How many did she give each neighbor? 28 ÷ 4 = 7
2. Mark and Melvin are brothers. They are saving for a puppy. So far they have each saved $4.75. The puppy costs $20. How much more do they need to save? $4.75 + $4.75 = $9.50 $20.00 - $9.50 = $10.50
3. The 4th grade class held a car wash to raise money to go on a special field trip. Each child needed to earn $36. If each child is paid $4 per car, how many cars does each child need to wash? $36 ÷ $4 = 9

In what place is the zero?

40 ones	90,835 thousands	10 ones
607 tens	205,624 ten thousands	409 tens
10,357 thousands	106 tens	5,032 hundreds
890 ones	706,318 ten thousands	50,927 ten thousands

*Write synonyms for the **bold** words to make a good sentence.*

yard 1. David, it is your turn to mow the lawn.

boat 2. That large ship is an aircraft carrier.

violet 3. Purple is my favorite color.

quick 4. A cheetah can run very fast.

carpet 5. Denise, please do not let your muddy shoes get on the new rug.

Circle the verbs.

1. An Ultra-Soaker-Supreme (is) a great water gun.
2. My friends and I (have) big water fights on hot afternoons.
3. We (run) and (hide) and (surprise) each other.
4. The cold water (feels) really good when I (am) hot and sweaty.

20

back

from *The Daddy Series for Little Folks*
by Howard Garis

Hal and Mab Blake lived with Daddy and Mother in a nice house in a small city. Uncle Pennywait and Aunt Lollipop lived with them. These were not their real names. Uncle Pennywait was called that because he so often said to Hal and Mab, "Wait a minute, and I'll give you a penny!" Aunt Lollipop was more often called Aunt Lolly. The reason she had such a queer name was because she was always telling the children to buy lollipops with the money Uncle Pennywait gave them. Lollipops, the children's aunt thought, were the best kind of candy for them. Perhaps she was right. Then there was Roly-Poly, the funny little poodle dog. Once when Daddy took Hal and Mab skating, Roly slid under the ice and was lost for a long, long time.

Hal and Mab just loved to go places with Daddy. They learned about the birds, trees and flowers. They had gone to the circus with him and sailing. They had hunted birds with a camera and taken pictures of them. They had many adventures each time they went out, and they learned many things.

Answer the questions about the story.

1. Why was Uncle Pennywait given his name? He was always asking the children to wait for a penny.
2. Why was Aunt Lolly given her name? She thought lollipops were the best candy.
3. Roly-Poly is the name of the Blake's (dog) insect brother sister
4. Write two sentences about something you have learned from your dad. Answers will vary.

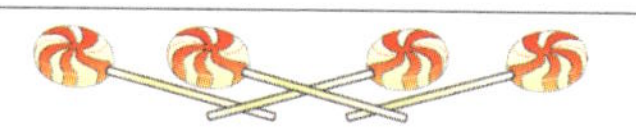

page 21 — front

Monday

Add.

62	21	65	87	16	24	74	51	94	80
+ 57	+ 85	+ 8	+ 44	+ 53	+ 9	+ 19	+ 37	+ 10	+ 35
119	106	73	131	69	33	93	88	104	115

Subtract to find how much change should be made. Draw coins to show the change.

Nancy bought some yarn for $1.47. She paid $2.00. $0.53 25¢ 25¢ 1¢ 1¢ 1¢	Larry bought an airplane kit for $5.75. He paid $6.00. $0.25 25¢
Greg bought a model ship for $4.14. He paid $4.25. $0.11 10¢ 1¢	Mary bought some fabric for $2.41. She paid $2.50. $0.09 5¢ 1¢ 1¢ 1¢ 1¢

Write a noun on each line to make an interesting story. Then circle the letters that should be capitalized.

i like to skate in my rollerblades on the driveway. sometimes William and Walter come over and we all skate together. we like to race each other and play tag. the cracks and the bumps in the driveway can be a problem, though.

Write the contraction on the line.

should have	should've	will not	won't
cannot	can't	let us	let's
they have	they've	who is	who's

21

page 22 — front

Tuesday

Multiply.

5	2	8	9	10	30	51	79	97	4
x 5	x 4	x 0	x 6	x 7	x 6	x 3	x 2	x 8	x 10
25	8	0	54	70	180	153	158	776	40

Color the correct amount of each shape.

1/2 3/4 5/6 9/12 2/3 4/6 8/18 6/8

Solve this story problem.

1. Andy feeds twenty-seven cows, five sheep and fourteen goats each morning. How many animals does he feed each morning? 27 + 5 + 14 = 46

Put periods in the sentences where they belong.

1. I live at 421 Redwood Cir. in Thompson, Mass.
2. Denise has never met Mrs. Jennifer G. Hartman.
3. Sammy has grown to be 4 ft. and 3 in. tall.
4. Holly visits Mrs. Teal on Wed. afternoons.
5. Dr. S. McDuff is my favorite dentist.

Circle the adjectives in the story.

Tanner's yellow foam airplane is a nice airplane. The long wings are adjustable and so are the tail fins. Tanner can make his plane fly in a straight line by adjusting the wings and tail a certain way. If he moves the wings another way, he can make his plane fly in a loop.

Sometimes Tanner puts a small weight on either the nose or the tail of the airplane. The small weight causes the airplane to fly differently. Tanner really enjoys experimenting with his yellow plane.

22

page 23 — front

Wednesday

Subtract.

$52.36	4,311	6,488	$39.81	2,442	6,013
- 4.75	- 547	- 620	- 3.99	- 776	- 555
$47.61	3,764	5,868	$35.82	1,666	5,458

Use the numbers to make four math facts.

8 72 9: 8 x 9 = 72; 9 x 8 = 72; 72 ÷ 8 = 9; 72 ÷ 9 = 8

3 12 4: 3 x 4 = 12; 4 x 3 = 12; 12 ÷ 3 = 4; 12 ÷ 4 = 3

9 36 4: 4 x 9 = 36; 9 x 4 = 36; 36 ÷ 4 = 9; 36 ÷ 9 = 4

Tell whether the sentence is **declarative**, **interrogative** *or* **exclamatory**.

declarative 1. It was fun to build a tree swing with Dad.
exclamatory 2. Don't run into the tree!
interrogative 3. Would you like a turn on the swing?
declarative 4. I like to try to climb the rope.
interrogative 5. Do you have a tall tree in your yard?

Put commas where they belong.

1. No, you may not sleep outside in this weather.
2. Kevin, you can play basketball very well.
3. Sarah, I am pleased with the way you have practiced the piano.
4. Laura, Peter, Walter and Julia went on the hike last Saturday.
5. My mother was born August 14, 1972, and my father was born the year before that.

??? *What is the capital of your state?* Answers will vary.

23

page 21 — back

Circle the operation(s) you need to do to solve the problem. Then solve the problem.

1. The Sinclairs decided to serve a buffet of fresh fruit at a party on Saturday. They bought 3 mega-melons at $7.75 each, strawberries for $7.25, apples for $4.95, pears for $6.15, and figs for $8.10. How much did they spend on fruit?

Step 1: + (x) ÷
Step 2: (+) x ÷
Answer: $49.70

2. Mrs. Thomas bought 4 pounds of apples for $2.75 per pound. How much did she pay for apples?

Step 1: + (x) ÷
Answer: $11.00

3. Blueberries are $3 a pint. How many pints can be bought for $12?

Step 1: + - x (÷)
Answer: 4

4. Regular watermelons are $4.95 each. Mega-melons are $7.75 each. How much less is a regular watermelon than a mega-melon?

Step 1: (-) x ÷
Answer: $2.80

5. Mrs. Gantry bought 5 pounds of apples for $2.75 per pound and 3 pounds of pears for $4.15 per pound. How much change did she get from two twenty dollar bills?

Step 1: + (x) ÷ — $2.75 x 5 = $13.75
Step 2: + (x) ÷ — $4.15 x 3 = $12.45
Step 3: (+) x ÷ — $13.75 + 12.45 = $26.20
Step 4: (-) x ÷ — $40.00 - 26.20 = $13.80
Answer: $13.80

page 22 — back

Answer the questions about the table of contents.

Contents

Chapter 1 - Bugs Are Everywhere! . . . 1
Chapter 2 - Not All Bugs Are Insects . . 5
Insect Characteristics . . . 6
Ticks . . . 8
Spiders . . . 11
Other Bugs . . . 15
Chapter 3 - Bug Homes . . . 20
Cities . . . 21
Gardens . . . 24
Farms . . . 29
Forests . . . 31
Waterways . . . 34
Mountains . . . 37
Deserts . . . 39
Chapter 4 - Bug Eating Habits . . . 42
Plant Eaters . . . 43
Animal Eaters . . . 46
Other Odd Foods . . . 49
Chapter 5 - Catching Bugs . . . 57
Using a Net . . . 58
Building Traps . . . 60
Chapter 6 - Bugs As Pets . . . 63
Making an Ant Farm . . . 64
Building a Wormery . . . 71
Bee Keeping . . . 80
Glossary . . . 95

1. Which chapter has the most sections? 3 The fewest? 1
2. To what page would you turn to read about bugs that live in creeks? 34
3. If you wanted to start a bee hive in your yard for fresh honey, what section should you read? Chapter 6, Bee Keeping

   On what page does this section begin? 80
4. If your family were going camping in the mountains and you wanted to see what kinds of bugs might be around your campsite, what section would you read? Chapter 3, Mountains

   On what page does this section begin? 37
5. What is a "Glossary"?
   a. a list of other good books to read
   b. a list of words found in the book and their definitions (circled)
   c. a large collection of pictures

If you would like to read an interesting bug book with lots of pictures (or you are going to have to make an insect collection next year for school and want to get started early) try *Bug Hunter* available online at www.summerbookcompany.com or by calling 877-684-8502.

page 23 — back

Look at the items in each row. Tell why the other items belong together and add another item to the group.

Example: banana apple pear grapes
Why? *The items are all fruits.* orange

1. pebble boulder stone — Why? The words are all names for rocks. gravel
2. plate cup spoon — Why? We use these things to eat. fork
3. robin cardinal wren — Why? These are kinds of birds. hawk
4. skirt shirt blouse tie — Why? We wear these. pants
5. Florida California Minnesota — Why? These are names of states. Texas
6. skates wagon bike — Why? These are toys with wheels. scooter
7. Barry Benjamin Bryan — Why? These boys' names begin with B. Bob
8. ice cream cottage cheese yogurt — Why? The foods are all dairy foods. butter
9. bunk twin double — Why? These are sizes or kinds of beds. queen
10. Stephanie Sarah Sylvia — Why? These girls' names begin with S. Stacy

front

page 24

Thursday

Divide.

3 ÷ 1 = 3 　 48 ÷ 6 = 8 　 5 ÷ 1 = 5 　 25 ÷ 5 = 5

0 ÷ 9 = 0 　 35 ÷ 5 = 7 　 4 ÷ 2 = 2 　 15 ÷ 3 = 5

6 ÷ 3 = 2 　 14 ÷ 7 = 2 　 6 ÷ 1 = 6 　 63 ÷ 9 = 7

Decide whether you should use inches, feet, or yards to measure these things.

the length of your driveway yards 　 the width of this page inches

how tall you are feet 　 the length of your shoe inches

the width of the living room feet 　 the height of the table feet

Number the words in each column in alphabetical order.

1 pansy	4 sheets	4 stand	1 beans
2 petal	2 pillows	3 skip	3 broccoli
4 purple	3 pink	1 saunter	2 beets
3 petunia	1 pajamas	2 sit	4 Brussels sprouts

Write the plural form of each word on the line.

lunch lunches 　 loaf loaves 　 foot feet

ax axes 　 bag bags 　 puppy puppies

Underline each subject once and each verb twice.

1. Nine boys practiced Hi-Li scoop ball in the empty lot in the neighborhood.
2. They caught and threw the ball with the scoops very well.
3. Tomorrow the boys will divide into teams and play a regular game.

24

back

Answer the questions.

1. A train going west passes by the station every two hours. If the most recent westbound train went by at 11:30 a. m., when should the station master expect the next westbound train?
1:30 p. m.

2. The Goldline Express travels from Empire City to Capital Landing in fourteen hours without stopping. If the train leaves Empire City at 7:00 a. m., when will it arrive in Capital Landing?
9:00 p. m.

3. The mail train stops at Tinytown at 8:12 a. m. every morning. It stops in Berryburg exactly thirty-five minutes later. Twenty minutes after that it stops in Hartsville. What time does the train stop in Hartsville each day?
9:07 a. m.

4. Mr. Clarendon takes a forty-five minute train ride home from work each day. If he arrives at 6:15 p. m., what time did his ride begin?
5:30 p. m.

5. Mr. and Mrs. Wiggins are going out west to see the Grand Canyon. The train trip is supposed to take twenty-three hours. If they leave on Wednesday at 6:00 p. m., what day and time will they arrive?
Thursday, 5:00 p. m.

6. The train trip from Gettysburg to Remington was supposed to take three hours, but it was delayed by twenty-three minutes. If the train was supposed to arrive at 8:45 p. m., what time did it actually pull into the station?
9:08 p. m.

front

page 25

Friday

Fill in the missing numbers.

5 + 5 = 10 　 9 x 7 = 63 　 7 + 9 = 16 　 8 x 5 = 40

6 + 6 = 12 　 7 x 8 = 56 　 6 + 9 = 15 　 6 x 5 = 30

9 + 7 = 16 　 5 x 8 = 40 　 7 + 6 = 13 　 6 x 7 = 42

Solve these story problems.

1. If it is 437 miles from Greenville, SC, to Pensacola, FL, how many miles is it for a round trip?
437 + 437 = 874

2. Bill is saving money to buy a $27 skateboard. So far he has $18. How much more does he need?
$27 - $18 = $9

3. How many days are in 3 years?
365 x 3 = 1,095

4. Mr. Greene drove 117 miles on a trip. Then he stopped for lunch and paid $4.37. After lunch he drove 193 more miles. How far did he drive in all?
117 + 193 = 310

Put quotation marks where they belong.

"What would you like to play today?" asked Elizabeth.

"I don't know," answered Grace. "We played hide and seek yesterday and house the day before that. What do you think we should do?"

"Why don't we draw with the sidewalk chalk?" suggested Elizabeth.

Add the missing punctuation and tell whether the sentence is a **declarative** *or* **interrogative** *sentence.*

declarative 1. Helen and Maggie like to toss the fuzzy ball.

declarative 2. They catch the ball with their velcro catchers.

interrogative 3. Who catches the ball the most, Helen or Maggie?

interrogative 4. Does this sound like fun to you?

declarative 5. The girls like to think of strange ways to catch the ball.

25

back

The White Giant
from *The Tale of Jolly Robin*

Jolly Robin was frightened. He saw a strange man. It was not Farmer Green or the hired man. This was a giant! He had big, black eyes and a great lump of a nose. The nose stuck out strangely from his face. He was dressed in all white and had an old, black hat. In one hand he held a stick. Jolly Robin was just about to go back to the farmhouse when he saw somebody come running toward the orchard. "Here's Johnnie Green!"

Jolly saw Johnnie Green stop and make an armful of snowballs. Then he went straight to the man in white. Johnnie began to shout, but the man in white did not move. Johnnie Green threw a snowball at the man. The snowball knocked off the man's hat. Jolly Robin was more surprised than ever because the man did not even turn his head!

"That's strange," said Jolly Robin to himself. "He must be asleep, but I should think he would wake up."

Answer the questions about the story.

1. What was the white giant? a snowman
2. List three clues that told you who the white giant was.
Answers will vary but should come from the story.
3. What animal is Jolly Robin? a bird
4. Johnnie Green is probably a(n) ______ man (boy) animal
How do you know? Answers will vary.

front

page 26

Monday

Add.

156	395	268	336	427	464	376
+ 477	+ 434	+ 189	+ 549	+ 285	+ 148	+ 597
633	829	457	885	712	612	973

Use each set of numbers to make four math facts.

8 17 9	5 13 8	6 13 7
8 + 9 = 17	5 + 8 = 13	6 + 7 = 13
9 + 8 = 17	8 + 5 = 13	7 + 6 = 13
17 - 8 = 9	13 - 5 = 8	13 - 6 = 7
17 - 9 = 8	13 - 8 = 5	13 - 7 = 6

What comes next?

3, 6, 9, 12, 15, 18, 21, 24, 27

5, 10, 15, 20, 25, 30, 35, 40, 45

7, 14, 21, 28, 35, 42, 49, 56, 63

Underline the words that need a capital letter.

1. last june grandpa and grandma lesley, who live in vermont, came to visit us.
2. the parade will start at the mall, travel down main street, and end at redlane park.
3. cindy and kathy are bob's and david's cousins.
4. "the star-spangled banner" is our national anthem.
5. what month comes before october?

Circle all the nouns in these sentences.

1. Ben loves to ride his scooter up and down the driveway and sidewalk.
2. The handles are covered in soft foam.
3. The back wheel has a great brake.
4. Ben has had the scooter for three years.
5. His friends Jerry and Mike also have scooters and the boys like to have races.

26

back

Answer the questions about the map.

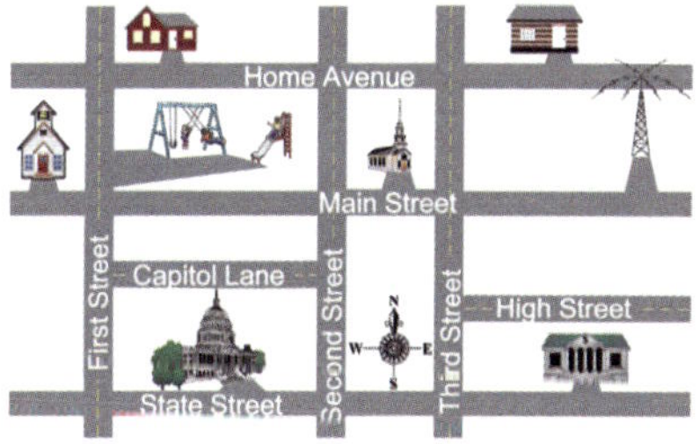

1. When driving from the bank to the capitol, which streets would you cross?
Second and Third Streets
2. The Jones family lives at the west end of Home Avenue. Each day Mr. Jones drives to his job at the radio tower by the shortest route. Does he drive on High Street?
no
3. Explain how to get from the school to the capitol building.
Turn left onto Main Street. Turn left onto First Street. Then turn right onto State Street.
4. Explain how to drive from the radio tower to the playground.
Turn left onto Main Street. Turn right on First Street. Turn right into the playground.

front

page 27

Tuesday

Multiply.

3 x 1 = 3 | 1 x 10 = 10 | 5 x 3 = 15 | 7 x 5 = 35
9 x 0 = 0 | 6 x 2 = 12 | 4 x 6 = 24 | 3 x 5 = 15
10 x 8 = 80 | 8 x 1 = 8 | 2 x 9 = 18 | 0 x 4 = 0

Write a mixed number to show how much has been shaded.

$2\frac{1}{2}$ $2\frac{2}{4}$ $1\frac{3}{4}$ $1\frac{1}{3}$

Put periods where they belong.

Mr. and Mrs. Timmons own the farm at the end of Rt. 99. They raise horses. Mr. Timmons is especially proud of his Tennessee Walkers. These horses are very beautiful and quite comfortable to ride. Mrs. Timmons raises miniature ponies as a hobby. Some people come and buy them and keep them in their houses as pets. I like to go to their farm and pet all the horses.

Write an adjective on the line to make a good sentence.

1. The purple flowers smelled very sweet.
2. The grasshopper quickly hopped into the thick weeds.
3. The camping lantern shone brightly.
4. Tired children were snuggled in their sleeping bags in the tent.
5. I like camping in the quiet woods.

??? Do you know how tall you are? Have someone measure you to the nearest inch.

I am ___ feet and ___ inches tall.

27

back

Find the names of twenty-four states in the puzzle. Be very careful. Some state names have been spelled incorrectly to try to trick you. Only circle the name of each state when it is spelled correctly.

R	V	S	X	W	N	P	E	N	N	E	B	R	A	S	C	A	R
H	O	O	E	T	I	N	E	T	N	E	N	T	O	H	I	O	N
O	K	U	M	U	E	S	V	N	E	E	B	E	E	D	P	R	O
D	L	T	W	O	N	N	C	E	N	X	W	R	V	X	E	A	R
E	A	H	E	N	N	O	N	O	R	S	A	Y	A	E	A	G	T
I	H	C	N	E	O	T	R	E	N	M	Y	S	O	S	D	O	H
S	O	A	W	W	R	R	A	T	S	S	O	L	U	R	K	N	D
L	M	R	Y	M	E	W	T	N	H	S	I	N	V	T	K	A	A
A	A	O	O	E	G	N	N	H	A	C	E	N	T	A	E	W	K
N	Y	L	M	X	O	N	E	V	A	D	A	E	N	W	N	H	O
D	U	I	I	I	N	P	N	E	W	J	E	R	S	E	Y	I	T
H	T	N	N	C	S	O	U	T	H	D	A	K	O	T	A	E	A
S	A	A	G	O	W	Y	O	M	M	I	N	G	I	L	A	N	D
A	H	R	N	E	W	H	A	M	P	S	H	I	R	E	I	W	V
W	A	S	H	I	N	G	T	O	N	P	E	N	S	Y	L	N	A
W	E	S	T	V	I	R	G	I	N	I	A	O	R	G	O	N	A

Montana	North Carolina	South Carolina	West Virginia
Nebraska	North Dakota	South Dakota	Wisconsin
Nevada	Ohio	Tennessee	Wyoming
New Hampshire	Oklahoma	Texas	
New Jersey	Oregon	Utah	
New Mexico	Pennsylvania	Vermont	
New York	Rhode Island	Washington	

front

page 28

Wednesday

Subtract and check by adding.

90	57	59	48	56	49	93	73
- 33	+ 33	- 11	+ 11	- 7	+ 7	- 20	+ 20
57	90	48	59	49	56	73	93

Put < or > in the circle.

8 + 1 > 2 + 2 | 13 - 5 > 11 - 4 | 13 - 6 > 3 + 1 | 13 - 8 < 4 + 5
8 + 6 < 7 + 9 | 10 - 5 > 12 - 9 | 11 - 8 > 1 + 1 | 14 - 7 < 6 + 3
5 + 6 > 8 + 2 | 17 - 9 < 11 - 2 | 17 - 8 < 3 + 9 | 10 - 6 > 1 + 2

*Write **our**, **your**, or **their** on the lines.*

1. Our house is going to be painted this summer before we move.
2. "Please raise your hand before speaking," said the teacher.
3. The children quickly licked their ice cream cones to keep them from dripping.
4. Please clean up your own room, George.
5. Many men wash and wax their cars on Saturday.

Circle the adjectives in the sentences.

1. The old basketball swished through the high net.
2. Four small boys played on the wide driveway in the early sunshine.
3. In the late afternoon, the older boys played an active game of basketball.
4. Kevin actually prefers to practice his free throws and other shots.
5. The boys like the best when dad has time to play with them.

Circle the correct word.

1. Mother, (may can) I go over to James' house for the afternoon?
2. Did you know that Penny (may can) tie her shoe all by herself?
3. For lunch I have (a an) sandwich and (a an) apple.
4. Do you have (a an) pair of scissors that I could borrow?
5. The (children's childrens') game was finished.
6. The (van's vans) motor is making a strange sound.

28

back

Fill in each blank with the best word from the bottom of the page.

George Washington Carver grew up to be a scientist who tried to understand every plant and animal and how it could be used. As a teacher at the Tuskegee Institute, he tried to teach his students all the things he learned and how to be good stewards of what had been given to them. He is, perhaps, best known for his work with peanuts.

Many southern farmers grew cotton every year. Each year the soil lost more of the vitamins and minerals needed by the cotton plants, so the plants were smaller and produced even less cotton. Dr. Carver encouraged the farmers to plant other crops to give the soil a rest. Few farmers listened until the boll weevil came and ate nearly all the cotton before it could be harvested. Then all the farmers wanted to grow something else. Dr. Carver encouraged them to grow peanuts.

Now the farmers had a new problem. People did not know what to do with peanuts, so no one wanted to buy them. Dr. Carver determined to solve this problem also. He locked himself in his laboratory with several baskets of peanuts. For days he stayed in his laboratory working. Finally he opened the door. He had many new products made from peanuts to show everyone. There was, of course, peanut butter as well as milk, margarine, Worcestershire sauce, rubbing oil, hand lotion, ink, glue and many other items. Everyone was amazed at all the things that could be done with a simple peanut.

He then wrote and talked to men who owned large factories to encourage them to use peanuts to make new products. The factories began buying lots of peanuts and the farmers' problem was solved.

buy	cotton	Tuskegee
factories	harvested	door
laboratory	peanuts	plants
problem	scientist	soil

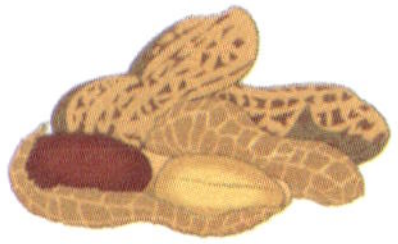

For an exciting but easy to read book about George Washington Carver, go to www.summerbookcompany.com/indivbooks/bcarver.htm or call 877-684-8502.

front

page 29

Thursday

Divide.

$7\overline{)51}$ = 7 r2 | $8\overline{)76}$ = 9 r4 | $6\overline{)41}$ = 6 r5 | $3\overline{)11}$ = 3 r2 | $5\overline{)29}$ = 5 r4 | $9\overline{)30}$ = 3 r3
$5\overline{)49}$ = 9 r4 | $7\overline{)61}$ = 8 r5 | $8\overline{)49}$ = 6 r1 | $4\overline{)19}$ = 4 r3 | $9\overline{)77}$ = 8 r5 | $2\overline{)20}$ = 10

Look at the graph to answer the following questions.

1. Who read the fewest books? Sandra
2. Who read more books, the boys or the girls? boys
3. Which two people read the same number of books? Kevin and Laura
4. How many more books did Laura read than Sandra? 4

Make the bold word plural and write it on the lines to make a good sentence.

wife 1. The men helped their wives put on their coats.
shirt 2. The store had long-sleeved shirts on sale.
daisy 3. The children ran through the field of daisies.
calf 4. All the calves stayed close to their mothers during the storm.
bush 5. A row of bushes is sometimes called a hedge.

Read the following story. Underline all the incomplete sentences.

One rainy day. Albert made a rubber band gun. From a kit. The gun was not hard to make. The gun is easy to cock and shoot. Fun shooting at a paper target. Sometimes Albert and his dad have a rubber band war. That is always lots of fun for Albert. Even if he loses.

29

back

Number each group of words in alphabetical order.

5 pine	2 yarn	3 barn	1 cab
4 pillow	5 younger	6 bring	5 car
2 penny	1 yard	4 best	4 canary
6 pony	4 yellow	2 bark	6 case
3 peony	6 yo-yo	1 bang	3 can
1 peep	3 yell	5 bill	2 call
1 head	2 joked	1 life	3 water
4 heat	4 joking	4 living	1 wait
2 hear	1 joke	3 liver	4 watt
3 heard	3 jokes	2 lift	2 waste

abcdefghijklmnopqrstuvwxyz

Circle the words that would be on the page between manager - maybe.

marble	man	mane	maple	make
mast	metal	march	male	map

Circle the words that would be on the page between bean - beverage.

beat	bead	beyond	be	bet
back	bitter	beside	best	berry
bewail	bewilder	betray	blister	bass

abcdefghijklmnopqrstuvwxyz

front

Friday

Write the Arabic numeral for the Roman numeral.
Remember: I = 1, V = 5, X = 10, L = 50 and C = 100.

XXV	25	CX	110	XLIV	44
VIII	8	XIV	14	CIX	109
XIV	14	XVIII	18	LXVI	66

Solve these story problems.

1. In Owasaka County it rained 114 days last year. How many days did it not rain?
   365 - 114 = 251
2. Jennifer has 24 slices of pizza. If 6 people share the pizza fairly (including Jennifer), how many slices can each person eat?
   24 ÷ 6 = 4
3. Jack was playing golf with his dad. The first hole is 425 yards long. On the first shot, Jack's ball went 230 yards. On the second shot, it went 150 yards. How many yards does Jack have left to go?
   230 + 150 = 380   425 - 380 = 45

Underline the correct word.

1. The Jones family packed the moving truck (theirselves, themselves).
2. I think that blue jacket hanging on the hook is (hers, her's).
3. Does (your, you're) dog know any tricks?
4. (Its, It's) not hard to believe that Jesus walked on water.
5. Mother said he must clean his room (himself, hisself).

*Tell whether the pairs of words are synonyms (**syn.**), homonyms (**hom.**) or antonyms (**ant.**).*

lady, woman	syn.	sick, well	ant.	tare, tear	hom.
hour, our	hom.	dead, alive	ant.	damp, moist	syn.
new, old	ant.	couch, sofa	syn.	son, sun	hom.
far, distant	syn.	threw, through	hom.	right, left	ant.

30

page 30

back

The Tiger
from *An Alphabet of Quadrupeds*

This very beautiful animal, called a tiger, lives in India. India is a very hot country in Asia. Tigers are fierce and will often kill men and animals much larger than themselves. They live in the woods and thickets, called jungles, where men hunt them. Tigers eat the flesh of animals which they kill. We have none in America except a few kept for show. The tiger is as big as a lion and has the shape of a cat, but much larger. He has a long tail and striped skin, covered with short hair. His skin is sometimes used for decoration. He is quite active and can jump far. Some tigers have been tamed, but he is a very sly and dangerous creature. He cannot be trusted.

Answer the questions about the paragraph.

1. What do tigers eat? plants (meat) tiger food
2. Where do tigers normally live? the zoo America (India)
3. Tiger skins are used for what? decoration
4. Why would a tiger be in the United States? for show
5. Write a synonym for the word *fierce*.
   ferocious

Color the tiger.

front

Monday

Add.

219 + 89	$4.57 + 0.78	514 + 59	139 + 247	$4.44 + 0.85	374 + 505	363 + 127
308	$5.35	573	386	$5.29	879	490

Subtract to find how much change should be made. Draw coins to show the change.

Jon's dad bought lunch for $4.23. He paid $5.00. $0.77 (25¢)(25¢)(25¢)(1¢)(1¢)	Carol's sister bought her a scarf for $3.91. She paid $4.00. $0.09 (5¢)(1¢)(1¢)(1¢)(1¢)
Ann's mom bought a few groceries for $9.74. She paid $10.00. $0.26 (25¢)(1¢)	Frank's brother bought him a belt for $5.03. He paid $5.25. $0.22 (10¢)(10¢)(1¢)(1¢)

Underline all the nouns.

1. The Hubers have a small rock wall for climbing on the side of their play set.
2. The boys pretend they are mountain climbers and brave adventurers.
3. Tim and Randy have strong hands and arms from climbing the rock wall.
4. The boys grip the little ledges with their fingers and toes.
5. When they were small, the boys thought the yellow rope was a challenge.

Circle the letters that should be capitalized. Put an X on any letter that is capitalized and should not be.

1. jack london wrote call of the wild and white fang.
2. mr. j. n. barnsworth is my Uncle on my Father's side of the Family.
3. have you ever Read on the banks of plum creek by laura ingalls wilder?
4. i love to go to see my Grandmother and see all the animals on her Farm.
5. sometimes easter comes in the Month of march and sometimes in april.

31

page 31

back

Put each group of items in order from first to last or smallest to largest.

3 May
1 January
5 August
2 March
4 June

4 October
2 April
5 December
3 July
1 February

5 sunset
1 dawn
2 morning
4 afternoon
3 noon

1 word
4 chapter
2 sentence
5 book
3 paragraph

1 roll over
5 run
3 crawl
4 walk
2 sit up

2 Tuesday
5 Saturday
3 Wednesday
4 Thursday
1 Monday

1 preschool
3 elementary school
2 kindergarten
4 high school
5 college

1 grit
4 boulder
2 pebble
5 mountain
3 stone

1 acorn
4 lumber
2 sapling
5 chair
3 tree

front

Tuesday

Multiply.

0 x 7	9 x 6	3 x 3	4 x 0	8 x 10	12 x 2	35 x 9	56 x 8	71 x 7	97 x 4
0	54	9	0	80	24	315	448	497	388

Draw a rectangle and color the correct amount.

$\frac{1}{3}$ $\frac{3}{4}$ $\frac{5}{6}$

$\frac{2}{5}$ $\frac{1}{2}$ $\frac{1}{4}$

Put periods where they belong.

1. The President of the United States lives in Washington, D.C.
2. She lives on the corner of Pine St. and Cherry Rd.
3. Dr. H. G. Benson is our family's dentist.
4. Mon. is the day my mother does the laundry, and Thurs. is the day she shops.
5. Mr. and Mrs. Thompson live four blocks away on Vine St.

Underline the adjectives in the sentences and draw an arrow to the word it describes.

1. Henry's blue aluminum bat is everyone's favorite.
2. The neighborhood boys play on a team with their dads.
3. This year the team bought new bases for the baseball diamond.
4. The dads mow the green grass and the boys smooth the brown dirt.
5. The mothers and their daughters provide cold drinks and yummy snacks.

??? If you add up the ages of everyone in your family will it equal more than 100?

32

page 32

back

Encyclopedias have many articles and provide much information. The articles are arranged in alphabetical order. Read the article below and answer the questions.

Marshmallows Marshmallows were first made from a plant that grew wild in marshes. It was called the mallow plant. Egyptians discovered the process of making this plant into a gooey treat. They used the sap from the plant and mixed nuts and honey with it.

Many years later the French decided to whip the sap by hand to make it fluffy. They also added cornstarch to make it stiff. They sold the treat in their candy stores. This process took a lot of time to do by hand. Candy makers started searching for an easier way to make marshmallows. Instead of using the mallow plant, candy makers began using gelatin, and America learned about the special treat.

A man named Alex Doumak made some more changes to the process. Marshmallow goo was put through tubes and then cut into pieces. Marshmallows became more popular and many people used them in different recipes.

Today Americans buy more marshmallows than any other country in the world. They buy more than ninety million pounds every year! The same ingredients - gelatin, corn syrup, starch, sugar and water - can be combined at home to make marshmallows. Salt and vanilla can be added for flavoring.

Answer the questions about the encyclopedia article.

1. What is the name of the plant from which marshmallows were first made?
   papyrus (mallow) sap candy
2. What was the first country to make marshmallows? Egypt
3. Using digits, write the number of pounds of marshmallows that Americans buy every year.
   90,000,000
4. Would the entry for marshmallows come before or after an entry on the month of March? before (after)
5. Number the words in the order you could find them in the encyclopedia.
   3 gelatin 1 candy 2 cornstarch 5 vanilla 4 sugar
6. Marshmallows could be found between which two entries?
   Maryland - Mice (Marborough - Mexico) Miracle - Miranda

front

page 33

Wednesday

Subtract.

603	977	530	721	874	543	635	714
- 353	- 266	- 307	- 188	- 479	- 167	- 48	- 275
250	711	223	533	395	376	587	439

Use the numbers to make four math facts.

3 18 6	6 48 8	5 20 4
3 × 6 = 18	6 × 8 = 48	4 × 5 = 20
6 × 3 = 18	8 × 6 = 48	5 × 4 = 20
18 ÷ 3 = 6	48 ÷ 6 = 8	20 ÷ 4 = 5
18 ÷ 6 = 3	48 ÷ 8 = 6	20 ÷ 5 = 4

Solve this story problem.

1. The Incredible Toy Palace has 194 stuffed animals, 217 dolls and 423 balls. How many of these three toys do they have?

194 + 217 + 423 = 834

Tell whether the sentence is **declarative, interrogative,** *or* **exclamatory**.

exclamatory 1. Watch out for that hornet's nest!
interrogative 2. Do you know how hot it is outside?
declarative 3. I like chocolate ice cream better than strawberry ice cream.
interrogative 4. Where is the dog?
declarative 5. Matt will be going into the fourth grade next year.

Put commas where they belong.

1. Mountain bikes, dirt bikes and speed bikes are all fun to ride.
2. Mike hopped on his bike, rode over to the store and bought some sugar.
3. Yes, I really like the way you cleaned your bicycle and polished it.
4. Megan, you must wear a bicycle helmet when you ride your bike on the street.

Summer Adventure

Have your parents help you find an old road or path near your town and take a bike hike with them. Offer to help pack and carry a picnic lunch for everyone.

33

back

Circle the words and phrases that describe insects.

four legs, two body parts, have bones, have feathers
have fur, many teeth, long hair, eight legs
have gills, (six legs), (have antennae), (most can fly)
(lay eggs), babies drink milk, (three body parts), have one eye

Circle the creatures that are insects.

front

page 34

Thursday

Divide.

0 ÷ 8 = 0	10 ÷ 2 = 5	1 ÷ 1 = 1	24 ÷ 3 = 8
8 ÷ 2 = 4	32 ÷ 8 = 4	0 ÷ 3 = 0	28 ÷ 4 = 7
6 ÷ 1 = 6	20 ÷ 5 = 4	6 ÷ 2 = 3	63 ÷ 7 = 9

Add.

19	285	92	331	596	38	482	33
22	555	73	468	371	15	298	57
+ 88	+ 127	+ 24	+ 229	+ 144	+ 41	+ 346	+ 13
129	967	189	1,028	1,111	94	1,126	103

Write the plural of each word on the line.

wrench wrenches	child children	car cars
fish fish	wife wives	shelf shelves
lady ladies	penny pennies	man men
wish wishes	deer deer	field fields

Look each word up in the dictionary. Copy the first definition onto the lines.

allegiance - Answers will vary.

deaf -

target -

scrub -

34

back

Write the homonyms in the crossword puzzle.

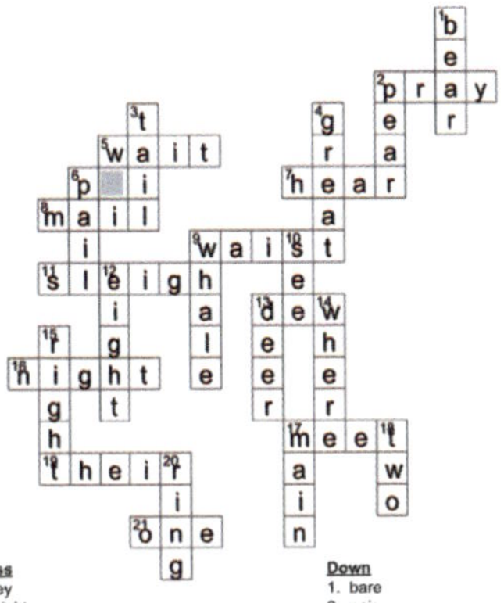

Across
2. prey
5. weight
7. here
8. male
9. waste
11. slay
13. do
16. knight
17. meat
19. there
21. won

Down
1. bare
2. pair
3. tale
4. grate
6. pale
9. wail
10. sea
12. ate
13. dear
14. wear
15. write
17. mane
18. too
20. wring

front

page 35

Friday

Underline the number in the tens place and circle the number in the thousands place.

32	46,875	129	5,034,872
7,205	19,634	90	5
1,681,304	9	586	739,530

Solve these story problems.

1. Dee bought six pizzas that were each $8.50 for a party. If she gave the delivery man $55.00, how much change should she get?

$8.50 x 6 = $51.00 $55 - $51 = $4

2. Virginia has two fruit pies to serve for dessert after dinner. If there are twelve people for dinner, into how many slices will she need to cut each pie?

12 ÷ 2 = 6

3. The Terrific Tree Trimmer Company has trimmed 32 trees a week for the last 3 weeks. How many trees have they trimmed in the last 3 weeks?

32 x 3 = 96

Put quotation marks where they belong.

"Men," said the coach, "We will be playing a very good team on Saturday, but I think we are ready for them."

After practice Barry said to Joseph, "We did not do very well against this team last year."

"I know," replied Joseph, "but the coach seems to think we will do better this year."

Circle possessive words (words that show ownership).

1. Is that (Barry's) soccer ball, or is it (Henry's)?
2. The (man's) new suit is gray, and the (woman's) coat is black.
3. The police sped after the man who took the (lady's) purse.
4. The tree house in the backyard is (Gary's) and (Tim's) special creation.
5. The pet (store's) dogs include four poodles and three cocker spaniels.

35

back

A Bear Story
by Edgar A. Guest

There was a bear -- his name was Jim,
An' children weren't askeered of him,
An' he lived in a cave, where he
Was confortubbul as could be,
An' in that cave, so my Pa said,
Jim always kept a stock of bread
An' honey, so that he could treat
The boys an' girls along his street.

An' all that Jim could say was "Woof!"
An' give a grunt that went like "Soof!"
An' Pa says when his grunt went off
It sounded jus' like Grandpa's cough,
Or like our Jerry when he's mad
An' growls at peddler men that's bad.
While grown-ups were afraid of Jim,
Kids could do anything with him.

One day a little boy like me
That had a sister Marjorie,
Was walking through the woods, an' they
Heard something "woofing" down that way,
An' they was scared an' stood stock still
An' wished they had a gun to kill
Whatever 'twas, but little boys
Don't have no guns that make a noise.

An' soon the "woofing" closer grew,
An' then a bear came into view,
The biggest bear you ever saw --
Ma's muff was smaller than his paw.
He saw the children an' he said:
"I ain't a-goin' to kill you dead;
You needn't turn away an' run;
I'm only scarin' you for fun."

An' then he stood up just like those
Big bears in circuses an' shows,
An' danced a jig, an' rolled about
An' said "Woof! Woof!" which meant
"Look out!" An' turned a somersault as slick
As any boy can do the trick.
Those children had been told of Jim
An' they decided it was him.

They stroked his nose when they got brave,
An' followed him into his cave,
An' Jim asked them if they liked honey,
They said they did. Said Jim: "That's funny.
I've asked a thousand boys or so
That question, an' not one's said no."
What happened then I cannot say
'Cause next I knew 'twas light as day.

Answer the questions about the poem.

1. In the first verse, *askeered* is what real word? scared
2. How should *confortubbul* be spelled? comfortable
3. How do you know that this story is not true? Answers will vary.

front

Monday

Add.

59	13	60	73	41	18	55	88	31	93
+ 6	+ 96	+ 48	+ 27	+ 79	+ 1	+ 36	+ 22	+ 66	+ 15
65	109	108	100	120	19	91	110	97	108

Use each set of numbers to make four math facts.

7 16 9	8 14 6	5 12 7
7 + 9 = 16	6 + 8 = 14	5 + 7 = 12
9 + 7 = 16	8 + 6 = 14	7 + 5 = 12
16 - 7 = 9	14 - 6 = 8	12 - 5 = 7
16 - 9 = 7	14 - 8 = 6	12 - 7 = 5

Underline all the nouns.

Owls are excellent hunters for several reasons. They have large eyes that see better than a human's eyes. They cannot turn their eyes in their heads the way people can, so they turn their necks. Owls also have special feathers on their wings which help the owls to fly almost silently. The feet of an owl are very strong and have sharp claws. All these things help make an owl a very good hunter.

Cross out the letters that should be capitalized and write a capital letter over them.

1. L S T R larry and his dad built a super jet rocket from a kit.
2. L S M P last saturday they went to a field at mentrose park and launched the rocket.
3. L larry was impressed by how high it went.
4. D L dad was quite pleased with how well larry had followed the directions when he built the rocket.
5. N L W W next larry and his dad plan to build a wonder winger later this summer.

☺ **Something Extra** ☺

On a separate page, write at least five good sentences telling about a vacation you have taken this summer. If you haven't been on vacation yet, write about a vacation you would like to take.

36

front

Tuesday

Multiply.

2 x 0 = 0	9 x 7 = 63	3 x 7 = 21	1 x 4 = 4
6 x 10 = 60	5 x 8 = 40	4 x 9 = 36	7 x 6 = 42
10 x 5 = 50	8 x 3 = 24	10 x 2 = 20	0 x 1 = 0

Write the correct fraction on the line.

3/12 3/9 5/11 6/13

9/18 15/18 4/9 2/4

Circle all the adjectives.

1. That pink flowered couch does not match the orange striped curtains.
2. The new curtains in Sarah's room have white lace around the edges.
3. Mr. Jacobs has a big shiny new truck that he washes every Saturday.
4. Those black and white penguins surely do look cute.
5. The bride had a lacy white dress and flowered veil.

Insert the missing periods and capital letters.

L M T J C last may t. j. and chad got a super bouncy ball as a gift. T W they like to bounce it back and forth to each other. when they bounce it on the brick sidewalk, the uneven bricks cause the ball to bounce in strange ways. T J t. j. likes to see if he can C bounce the ball right past chad.

37

front

Wednesday

Subtract.

$67.59	1,895	3,362	$77.58	4,579	4,015	$86.73
- 8.38	- 226	- 484	- 1.51	- 656	- 890	- 4.31
$59.21	1,669	2,878	$76.07	3,923	3,125	$82.42

Put < or > in the circle.

3 + 2 < 4 + 2	9 x 2 < 3 x 7	7 + 0 < 8 + 2	4 x 6 < 9 x 6
8 + 7 > 5 + 9	7 x 7 > 9 x 3	7 + 4 > 2 + 8	3 x 7 < 6 x 6
0 + 5 > 2 + 2	3 x 8 < 5 x 5	6 + 3 < 9 + 4	8 x 7 < 8 x 9

Circle the words that show ownership. Underline the verbs.

The twins, Sam and Dan built a small reading loft in a tree. Sam's favorite time of day for reading is in the morning. Dan's favorite time is in the late afternoon. The boys' parents are glad that Sam and Dan like books.

The boys' loft is used for other things besides reading. It is Sam's favorite lookout when playing army. The high loft is Dan's best perch when using his binoculars.

Place commas where they belong.

1. Thomas, please do not let your wet umbrella drip on the carpet.
2. Susan's aunt lives in Grafton, WV.
3. Billy, I need you to mow the lawn, clean your room and take out the trash.
4. The Declaration of Independence was signed in Philadelphia, PA.
5. Beans, peas, carrots and beets are all vegetables.

Write the two words for these contractions.

couldn't	could not	you've	you have
I'm	I am	she'll	she will
we're	we are	it's	it is
they're	they are	you'd	you would

38

page 36

back

Choose the operation or operations you would need to do to find the answer. You do not have to solve the problems unless you want to for extra practice.

Frank's Farriers

Your horse shod while you wait

1. Frank can put on a horse shoe in eighteen minutes. If a man has a team of four horses that all need new shoes, how long will it take Frank to finish them all?

Step 1: add subtract (multiply) divide

Step 2: add subtract (multiply) divide

2. Frank charges $75 to shoe a horse. How much is that per hoof?

add subtract multiply (divide)

3. Frank's brother, Fred, is just learning to shoe horses. It takes him five minutes more per hoof than it takes Frank. How much longer does it take Fred to shoe a horse?

add subtract (multiply) divide

4. Horse shoes cost Frank $4.75 each, but he charges his customers $5.50. How much money is Frank making on each shoe?

add (subtract) multiply divide

5. Frank charged Mr. Hodgekins $75 to shoe his horse and $5.50 each for four extra horse shoes. How much did Mr. Hodgekins owe?

Step 1: add subtract (multiply) divide

Step 2: (add) subtract multiply divide

6. All the horses in the Arabian Club were brought to Frank for new shoes before they were in the parade. Frank worked extra fast and finished a horse every seventy minutes. If he worked for five hours straight, how many horses did he completely finish?

Step 1: add subtract (multiply) divide

Step 2: add subtract multiply (divide)

7. Frank ordered thirty-six small shoes, eighty-four medium shoes, and sixteen large shoes. How many shoes did he order in all?

(add) subtract multiply divide

8. Frank is forty-eight years old and has been in business for twenty-seven years. He hopes to retire when he is sixty-five. How many more years will he be working?

add (subtract) multiply divide

page 37

back

Cheerfulness
by Marian Douglas

There is a little maiden -
Who is she? Do you know?
Who always has a welcome,
Wherever she may go.

Her face is like the May time,
Her voice is like a bird's;
The sweetest of all music
Is in her lightsome words.

Each spot she makes the brighter,
As if she were the sun;
And she is sought and cherished
And loved by everyone;

By old folks and by children,
By lofty and by low:
Who is this little maiden?
Does anybody know?

You surely must have met her.
You certainly can guess;
What! I must introduce her?
Her name is Cheerfulness.

Answer the questions about the poem.

1. What is a maiden? a boy (a girl) an animal
2. Is this poem describing a particular girl named Cheerfulness? yes (no)

   Who is this poem describing? Answers will vary.
3. Why do people like her so much? She makes everyone happier.
4. What does *cherished* mean? loved tenderly
5. Could this poem be describing you today? yes no

   Answers will vary.

page 38

back

Cross out the item in each row that does not belong. Then tell why the other items belong together.

Example: candy apple stop sign ~~the ocean~~ fire engine

Why? *The other items are usually red.*

1. markers crayons ~~scissors~~ pencil

   Why? We write or draw with the other items.
2. gerbil ~~cat~~ mouse hamster

   Why? The others are rodents.
3. swimming canoeing rafting ~~hiking~~

   Why? These sports require water.
4. baby ~~mother~~ infant newborn

   Why? A mother is an adult; the others are not.
5. big large huge ~~round~~

   Why? These are adjectives telling size.
6. Paul Peter ~~Priscilla~~ Patrick

   Why? These are boys' names.
7. ~~mittens~~ hat hood cap

   Why? We wear these on our heads.
8. stove oven ~~mixer~~ microwave

   Why? We cook with these.
9. mane ~~scales~~ tail hoof

   Why? A horse does not have scales.
10. quickly slowly neatly ~~tired~~

    Why? These words end in *ly*.

front

page 39

Thursday

Divide.

0 ÷ 8 = 0 | 10 ÷ 2 = 5 | 1 ÷ 1 = 1 | 24 ÷ 3 = 8
8 ÷ 2 = 4 | 32 ÷ 8 = 4 | 0 ÷ 3 = 0 | 28 ÷ 4 = 7
6 ÷ 1 = 6 | 20 ÷ 5 = 4 | 6 ÷ 2 = 3 | 63 ÷ 7 = 9

Fill in the blanks.

36 inches = 3 feet | 2 yards = 6 feet | 3 yards = 9 feet
9 feet = 3 yards | 6 feet = 2 yards | 2 feet = 24 inches
24 inches = 2 feet | 3 feet = 36 inches | 1 yard = 36 inches

Write the plural form of the word on the line.

moose moose | daddy daddies | truck trucks
leaf leaves | sheep sheep | ax axes
arm arms | church churches | bush bushes
pass passes | nail nails | reply replies

Write **complete** *on the line if the words make a complete sentence. Write* **incomplete** *if the words do not make a complete sentence.*

incomplete 1. A pool of cool, sparkling water.
complete 2. Jim can swim like a fish.
incomplete 3. Splashing and playing together.
complete 4. Shannon dives very well.
incomplete 5. Relief from summer heat.

Something Special
Time is the most precious thing a person has. Give some of your time to someone else today by helping them do a job more quickly.

39

back

Hint Hunter

Five neighbors on Valley View Road have different jobs in the community. Mr. Hardy's job is extremely noisy, so he wears ear plugs every day. Mr. Lawson has helped with the evening news every week night for the last twelve years. Mr. Eavers really enjoys his job. He loves the rush and hurry and the chance to save lives and property. He trains carefully all the time, so he will not get hurt in dangerous situations. Mr. Finch started learning his trade when he was a boy helping his dad. He thinks helping to build homes for other people is a really special job. Mr. Green's favorite time of day is when he gets to help children cross the street after school. Which man has which job?

Mr. Eavers
Mr. Finch
Mr. Greene
Mr. Hardy
Mr. Lawson

front

page 40

Friday

Fill in the missing numbers.

5 + 5 = 10 | 9 x 7 = 63 | 7 + 9 = 16 | 8 x 5 = 40
6 + 6 = 12 | 7 x 8 = 56 | 6 + 9 = 15 | 6 x 5 = 30
9 + 7 = 16 | 5 x 8 = 40 | 7 + 6 = 13 | 6 x 7 = 42

Solve these story problems.

1. Farmer Joe has to deliver 8 dozen eggs to his customers today. How many eggs will he be delivering?
8 x 12 = 96

2. Laura has 23 paper dolls and Michelle has 17. How many more does Laura have?
23 - 17 = 6

3. Ben has 14 conch shells, 12 clam shells and 18 periwinkle shells in his shell collection. How many shells does he have altogether?
14 + 12 + 18 = 44

Write a homonym on the line for the bold word.

wait 1. When you stand on a scale, it tells you your weight.
hair 2. A hare is another name for a rabbit.
so 3. A tailor is a man who will sew for money.
new 4. Andrea knew the answers to all the questions on the test.
knight 5. It is quite dark at night.

Circle the correct word or words.

1. Do you believe (there is, there are) a dog who can write?
2. I think he (has, have) finished his chores cheerfully.
3. (There is, There are) several low swings on the swing set.
4. The swing set (are, is) one of the favorite places for children to play on the playground.
5. Do you know how many stars (there is, there are) in the sky?

What is the best piece of playground equipment you have ever played on in your whole life?

40

back

Little Goody Two Shoes
Adapted from *Goldsmith*

Margery's parents had died. She and her brother were very poor and ragged. Though Tommy had two shoes, Margery had only one. They had nothing, poor little things, but what kind people gave to them. Each night they lay on hay in a barn.

Mr. Smith was a very good man. Although he was poor, he took the children home to live with him. Mr. Smith had a friend who was a wealthy man. When he heard about Margery and Tommy, this man gave Mr. Smith some money. It was to buy Margery a new pair of shoes and Tommy a new suit of clothes.

The next morning the shoemaker came in with Margery's new shoes. She put them on in great glee and ran out to Mrs. Smith. Margery cried, "Two shoes, two shoes. Goody, two shoes!" She did this to all the people she met, so that soon she was known far and wide as Goody Two Shoes.

Dear little Margery saw how good and wise Mr. Smith was. She thought it was because he read so many books. Margery wished so badly to learn to read. She would borrow books from the school children and sit down and read and read. Very soon she could read better than any of her playmates.

Margery enjoyed her books so much that she wished everybody else could read too, so she formed a plan.

First, she made letters out of bits of wood with her knife. She worked and worked until there were ten sets of small letters and six sets of the big letters. She then made the little tots spell words with her wooden letters. Each morning, with her basket full of wooden letters, Margery went around from house to house. The little children learned to read very quickly.

At last Margery grew up and was given a real school to teach. She still used her little wooden letters and made the children use them to spell the words.

Another gentleman, Sir Charles Jones heard of Margery's goodness. He offered her a home if she would teach his daughter. In fact he finally fell in love with Margery, and they were married in a big church.

She did not forget the children, you may be sure. A house in the village was fitted up as a school, and all the boys and girls were taught to read and write.

Answer the questions about the story.

1. Why were Margery and her brother all alone in the world? Their parents had died.
2. At the beginning of the story, Margery had how many shoes? 0 (1) 2
3. Margery believed that Mr. Smith was wise because he did what? He read so many books.
4. How many sets of letters did she make altogether? 6 10 (16) 26
5. Do you think the children enjoyed learning from Margery? (yes) no
Why? Answers will vary.
6. Why is this story called "Little Goody Two Shoes"? because of what she said when she got her shoes

front

page 41

Monday

Add.

245	547	167	588	379	238	328
+ 365	+ 225	+ 439	+ 254	+ 474	+ 158	+ 486
610	772	606	842	853	396	814

Subtract to find how much change should be made. Draw coins to show the change.

Mark owes Peter $2.15. He gave him $2.25. $0.10 (10¢)	Kathy owes Ginger $0.40. She gave her $0.50. $0.10 (10¢)
Laura owes Danielle $1.70. She gave her two dollars. $0.30 (25¢) (5¢)	Tim owes Robert $8.13. He gave him $8.25. $0.12 (10¢) (1¢) (1¢)

Circle the letters that should be capitalized.

1. is aunt mary's birthday in september or october?
2. mr. bob kepler and mrs. dot richardson are brother and sister.
3. on our vacation we are going to visit jamestown and yorktown, virginia.
4. does riverside lane actually run right along the side of black lick river?
5. my dad thinks my mom is the most wonderful woman in the world.

Put a ✓ over the underlined word if it is a noun. Put an **X** *over the word if it is not a noun.*

Randall loves his skateboard. He has learned to do several tricks on it. When Randall first started using his skateboard, he often forgot to wear his helmet, knee pads and elbow pads. After falling down and getting all scraped up a few times, Randall realized it was important to wear his safety gear whenever he was using his skateboard.

41

back

Answer the questions about the map.

1. After each state, write its letter from the map.

California	C	Oklahoma	D
Florida	J	Pennsylvania	G
Georgia	I	Texas	E
Michigan	F	Virginia	H
Montana	B	Washington	A

2. Name two states that border the Atlantic Ocean. ME, NH, MA, RI, CT, NY, NJ, DE, MD, VA, NC, SC, GA, FL
3. Name two states that border Canada. ME, NH, VT, NY, MI, MN, ND, MT, ID, WA
4. Name two states that border the Pacific Ocean. WA, OR, CA

front

page 42

Tuesday

Multiply.

10 × 6	4 × 3	1 × 5	7 × 7	9 × 10	3 × 9	22 × 8	45 × 4	68 × 2	86 × 1
60	12	5	49	90	27	176	180	136	86

Color in the circles.

$1\frac{1}{4}$ $2\frac{1}{2}$ $2\frac{3}{4}$ $1\frac{2}{3}$

Place periods and capital letters where they belong in the paragraph.

On a rainy day, a paddle and ball is a good toy. You can play several different games with it. You can try to catch the ball in all the holes in order. For another game, you and a brother or sister can pick a number and see who reaches it first. If you use your imagination, you can think of all kinds of fun things to do with a ball and a paddle.

Write an adjective before each word to describe it. Try not to use the same word twice.

song bird	new house	sweet girl
red car	tall boy	porcelain dish
green apple	smart man	leaning tree
soft bed	furry cat	blue pen

front

page 43

Wednesday

Subtract and check by adding.

60 − 24 = 36	36 + 24 = 60	82 − 15 = 67	67 + 15 = 82	68 − 29 = 39	39 + 29 = 68	95 − 17 = 78	78 + 17 = 95

Use the numbers to make four equations.

7 63 9	8 56 7	5 30 6
7 × 9 = 63	7 × 8 = 56	5 × 6 = 30
9 × 7 = 63	8 × 7 = 56	6 × 5 = 30
63 ÷ 7 = 9	56 ÷ 7 = 8	30 ÷ 5 = 6
63 ÷ 9 = 7	56 ÷ 8 = 7	30 ÷ 6 = 5

Write the type of sentence called for by the bold word.

declarative Answers will vary.

exclamatory

interrogative

Place commas where they belong.

1. Marcie's father was born on July 24, 1962, in Chicago.
2. Yes, Calvin, you may ride your bike in the driveway.
3. No, Dr. Barton is not in the office right now.
4. On October 12, 2019, Mrs. Elliot will be one hundred years old.
5. Leigh, will you please call Mrs. Fisher and see if she is ready to leave?

Underline the subject once and the verb twice.

1. After the ball game was over, my family went to a restaurant for dinner.
2. During dinner, we celebrated my brother's home run.
3. My brother's team, the Parrots, has not had a winning season.
4. Have you ever hit a home run?

front

page 44

Thursday

Divide.

6)53	10)64	3)7	5)18	2)2	8)29
8 r5	6 r4	2 r1	3 r3	1	3 r5

3)17	5)38	10)21	9)40	10)75	7)24
5 r2	7 r3	2 r1	4 r4	7 r5	3 r3

Look at the graph to answer the questions.

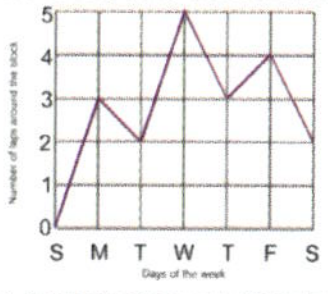

1. Which day did Michael run the most laps? Wednesday
2. Did he run more laps Mon.-Wed. or Thurs.-Sat.? Mon. - Wed.
3. Which day did he run the same number of laps as he ran on Monday? Thursday
4. Which day of the week did Michael rest? Sunday
5. How many laps did Michael run during the whole week? 19

Number the words in each column in alphabetical order.

4 rope	3 jump	3 skip	3 hop
1 road	4 just	2 sing	2 help
2 roam	1 jacks	1 scrap	1 handle
3 rode	2 jail	4 step	4 hurry

Write the plural form of the words on the lines.

knife knives	woman women	fish fish
puppy puppies	ash ashes	ditch ditches
airplane airplanes	plate plates	goose geese
elf elves	city cities	sheep sheep

back

page 42

Use the information below to answer the questions.

Carl's Camping

If we don't have it, you don't need it!

Two Man Tent - Quality lightweight tent easily sets up at night. Extra waterproof floor. Green or brown. $68.98

Family Tent - This great tent is so high even dad can stand up inside. Sleeps 6. $95.99 Extra rain cover $24.95

Bright Lantern . . $17.25
Firewood Ax . . . $15.85
Super Shovel . . . $12.45
Three Tool Set . . . $35.95

Carry all your gear in this sturdy back pack. The bedroll will keep you warm even on cold nights.
Backpack $31.49
Bedroll $19.88
Backpack and Bedroll . $49.50

1. How much is the family tent with the rain cover? $120.94
2. Thomas paid $90 when he bought the two-man tent and the lantern. How much change did he receive? $3.77
3. How much more is it if you buy the lantern, ax, and shovel separately than if you buy the three piece tool set? $9.60
4. All twelve of the boys in the Super Scout Club wanted to buy a backpack and bedroll set before the club's next camping trip. Mr. Carl, the owner, said he would give each boy a $5 coupon. How much is a backpack and bedroll set when a boy uses his coupon? $44.50
5. If all twelve boys use their coupons, how much money will they save? $60.00
6. Mr. Penny saw an ad in the paper saying that he could save $10 if he bought the family tent and the three piece tool set on Saturday. What would be the total for those items on Saturday? $121.94

back

page 43

Draw a line from Beethoven to his instrument, the piano. Do not go "through" any other instrument to get there.

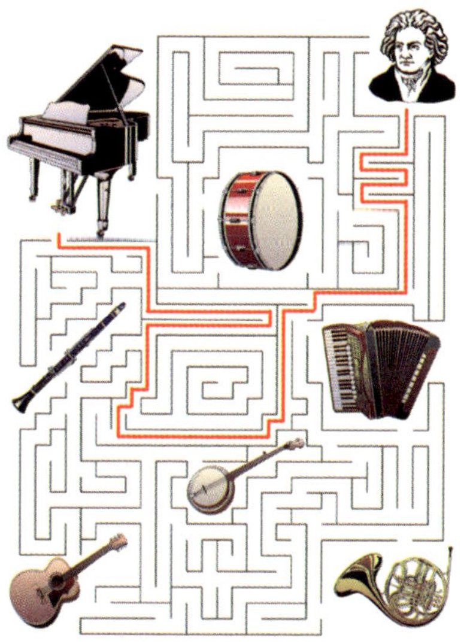

back

page 44

Follow the directions to change one word into another.

summertime

1. Change each *e* to an *a*. summartima
2. Change each *m* to a *v*. suvvartiva
3. Switch the last two letters. suvvartiav
4. Delete the *s*. uvvartiav
5. Change the *u* to an *o*. ovvartiav
6. Switch the *o* and the last *a*. avvartlov
7. Change the last *v* to an *n*. avvartion
8. Change the *r* to a *c*. avvaction
9. Put the first *a* after the *c*. vvacation
10. Delete the first letter. vacation

Draw a picture of the answer.

Answers will vary.

front

page 45

Friday

Fill in the missing numbers. Example: If 4 + 7 = 11, then 7 + 4 = 11.

If 7 + 5 = 12, then 5 + 7 = 12 — If 8 x 7 = 56, then 7 x 8 = 56

If 6 + 8 = 14, then 8 + 6 = 14 — If 5 x 3 = 15, then 3 x 5 = 15

If 2 + 9 = 11, then 9 + 2 = 11 — If 6 x 4 = 24, then 4 x 6 = 24

Solve these story problems.

1. Mr. Pine grew 47 tomatoes last year, and Mr. Ed grew 39. How many more did Mr. Pine grow?
   47-39=8
2. The Saluda River is 2 times as long as the Pee Dee River which is 34 miles long. The Pee Dee River is 27 feet wide, but the Saluda River is only 24 feet wide. How long is the Saluda River?
   34 x 2 = 68

Put quotation marks where they belong in the sentences.

"What kind of kite is that, Carl?" asked Samuel. "I have never seen one like it."

"I don't know what the name of it is, but Dad and I built it from straws, string, and tissue paper," replied Carl. "Let me show you how well it flies!"

Underline the verb(s). Circle the subject(s).

1. Wednesday is the day before Thursday.
2. That parrot talks and squawks all day.
3. Do you know where the boxes were placed?
4. Penny and Polly are identical twins.
5. Will you wash the car for me, Frank?

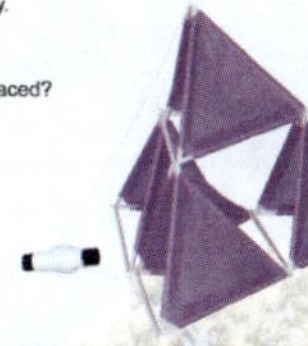

Extra Project

Can you look at the picture and figure out how to build a kite like this one?

45

back

The Bear and the Children
from *McGuffey's Second Eclectic Reader*

In the parlor of an inn in a small town, sat a man who had been going around with a bear. He was waiting for his supper, and the bear was tied up in the yard.

Up in the attic, three little children were playing together. The oldest might have been six years old. The youngest was not more than two.

Stump! Stump! Stump! Someone was coming up the stairs. The door flew open suddenly, and there stood the great, shaggy bear. He had gotten tired of waiting and had found his way to the stairs.

The children were badly frightened. Each one crept into a corner, but the bear found them all, smelled their clothes, and did not hurt them. "This must be a great dog," they said, and they began to pat him.

Then the bear lay down on the floor. The youngest boy climbed on his back, hid his head in the shaggy fur, and played "hide and seek."

When the oldest boy took his drum and began to strike it, then the bear rose on his hind legs and danced. At that the children gave a merry shout.

The two younger boys took their wooden guns, and gave the bear one. Away they all marched around the room.

Now the frightened mother of the children came to the door. But the youngest boy shouted joyfully. "See, we are playing soldiers!"

Then the bear's master came running up, and took the bear away.

Answer the questions about the story.

1. What do you think you would have done if you were one of the children?
   Answers will vary.
2. Write a synonym for the word *merry*. happy
3. What do you think your mother would have done if she were the mother in the story?
   Answers will vary.

front

page 46

Monday

Add.

455	$5.38	194	299	$5.34	164	276
+ 216	+ 0.97	+ 329	+ 425	+ 3.07	+ 418	+ 567
671	$6.35	523	724	$8.41	582	843

Use each set of numbers to make four math facts.

9 14 5 — 9 + 5 = 14, 5 + 9 = 14, 14 - 9 = 5, 14 - 5 = 9

6 11 5 — 5 + 6 = 11, 6 + 5 = 11, 11 - 5 = 6, 11 - 6 = 5

4 12 8 — 4 + 8 = 12, 8 + 4 = 12, 12 - 4 = 8, 12 - 8 = 4

What comes next?

8, 16, 24, 32, 40, 48, 56, 64, 72

9, 18, 27, 36, 45, 54, 63, 72, 81

Circle all the nouns.

Whales are not fish. They are mammals. Fish breathe through gills but whales breathe through a hole on the top of their heads. Fish are covered with scales. Whales are not covered with scales but skin. Whales do not lay eggs like fish. Instead their babies are born the same way that kittens and puppies are born.

Correct the capitalization.

1. R H G robert h. goddard is considered to be T F M R "the father of modern rocketry."
2. T S the saturn rocket was used to launch the moon-going astronauts.
3. M P T mr. paul timmons is the president of our local rocket club.
4. I M T i like to hear mr. timmons talk about his model rockets.
5. E S G R C every month, on the second saturday, the gainesville rocket club meets to launch rockets if it is not raining.

46

back

Make a new word and write it on the line. There may be more than one word that can be made from the letters. Any good word is a fine answer.

1. bird - d = rib
2. fail + r = frail
3. gush - s = hug
4. leaf + r = flare
5. meat - m = eat, ate, tea
6. earth + s - h = rates, stare, tears
7. heel - e + d = held
8. absurd + i - u = braids
9. word + a - o = ward, draw
10. smear - m + w = swear, wares, wears
11. kidney + l - y = kindle, linked
12. tours - s + e = route, outer

front

page 47

Tuesday

Multiply.

1 x 0 = 0 — 8 x 5 = 40 — 10 x 9 = 90 — 6 x 3 = 18

2 x 10 = 20 — 9 x 8 = 72 — 5 x 6 = 30 — 3 x 4 = 12

7 x 2 = 14 — 4 x 1 = 4 — 0 x 3 = 0 — 7 x 0 = 0

Write the fraction on the line.

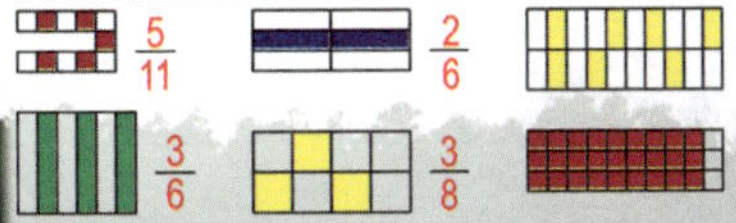

$\frac{5}{11}$ $\frac{2}{6}$ $\frac{7}{20}$ $\frac{3}{6}$ $\frac{3}{8}$ $\frac{27}{30}$

Put periods in the paragraph where they belong.

Bocce ball is a fun game to play. The small ball, called the jack, is thrown out into the grass. Then each team takes a turn throwing a ball. The teams try to get their balls closest to the jack. The teams keep taking turns until all the balls have been thrown. Points are scored by the team with their balls closest to the jack.

Underline each adjective and draw an arrow to the word it describes.

1. That new coat and long scarf do not match at all.
2. The busy ant hurried away to his anthill with a large crumb of bread.
3. Why is that small box on the table in the kitchen?
4. It is nice to see the green grass, blue sky and pretty flowers on a sunny day.
5. Red roses and white carnations make a lovely bouquet.

47

back

Tom Thumb
An English Fairy Tale

Tom never grew any larger than a man's thumb, so many interesting things happened to him. One day his mother was mixing a pudding. Tom leaned over the edge of the bowl to see how it was made. He slipped, and in he went, head first. His mother did not see him fall and kept stirring the pudding. Tom could not see nor hear, but he kicked and kicked inside the pudding. The pudding moved and tossed about. His mother was afraid. She did not know what to think. "Something must be wrong with it," she said.

She went to the window to throw the pudding out. Just then a poor beggar was passing by the house. "Here is a pudding you may have, if you like," said Tom's mother. The beggar thanked her and put it into his basket. He had not gone very far, when Tom got his head out of the pudding and shouted in a shrill voice: "Take me out! Take me out!"

The poor beggar was so frightened that he dropped his basket, pudding and all, and ran off as fast as he could. Tom crawled out of the pudding, climbed out of the basket, and ran home. His mother washed him and put him to bed.

Not long afterward, his mother took him with her when she went to milk the cow. She tied him to a wisp of hay so that he would not get lost. When Tom's mother was not looking, the cow took the wisp of hay into her mouth. She began to chew and chew. Tom began to jump about and shout. He frightened the cow so that she opened her great mouth and out Tom jumped. Then Tom's mother took him in her apron and ran with him to the house. He was not hurt in the least.

One time Tom was in the field helping his father. "May I drive the horse home?" asked Tom. "I could stand in the horse's ear and tell him which way to go," said Tom. So his father put him in the horse's ear, and he drove safely home. "Mother!" cried Tom, but when Tom's mother came out, she could not see him and began to be afraid. "Here I am in the horse's ear. Please take me down," said Tom.

His mother lifted him gently down, kissed him, and gave him a blackberry for his supper. Tom's father made him a whip out of a straw. Tom tried to drive the cows, but he fell into a deep ditch. There a great bird saw him and thought he was a mouse. The bird seized Tom in her claws and carried him toward her nest. As they were passing over the sea, Tom got away and fell into the water, where a great fish swallowed him.

When the fish was caught, it was so big that it was sent to the king. When the cook cut open the fish, out jumped Tom Thumb. Tom was brought before the king and told his story.

The king grew very fond of Tom. He took Tom with him wherever he went. If it began to rain, Tom would creep into the king's pocket and sleep until the rain was over. The king had a new suit made for Tom and gave him a needle for a sword. A mouse was trained for Tom to ride.

One day, as they were going hunting, a cat jumped out and caught Tom's mouse. Tom drew his sword and tried to drive the cat away. The king ran to help poor Tom, but the little mouse was dead, and Tom was scratched and bitten. Tom was put to bed, but he did not die. No indeed! He was soon well again and fought many brave battles and did many brave deeds to please the king.

On a separate sheet of paper, write about another adventure that could have happened to Tom. Answers will vary.

front

Wednesday

Subtract.

933	727	928	545	841	602	820	661
- 496	- 382	- 190	- 498	- 257	- 91	- 354	- 229
437	345	738	47	584	511	466	432

Put < or > in the circle.

56 ÷ 8 < 40 ÷ 5	17 - 9 > 35 ÷ 7	48 ÷ 8 > 11 - 6	18 - 9 > 14 - 6
63 ÷ 7 > 54 ÷ 9	12 - 5 < 56 ÷ 7	42 ÷ 6 > 11 - 5	13 - 7 < 16 - 8
64 ÷ 8 < 54 ÷ 6	13 - 8 < 63 ÷ 9	30 ÷ 5 < 16 - 7	14 - 5 > 16 - 9

*Write **us**, **you**, or **them** on the line.*

1. It was very nice of __them__ to share their sand toys with __us__.
2. Have __you__ ever ridden a little boat like this at the sea shore?
3. The rain got __us__ all wet because we didn't have an umbrella.
4. Be careful when __you__ are out in those waves!
5. Kelly, did __you__ thank __them__ for sharing their things with us?

Place commas where they belong.

1. Buffalo, NY, is about one hundred miles from Erie, PA.
2. Mr. Little likes ham, cheese, onions and green peppers in his omelette.
3. Do you know who was born on April 2, 1968?
4. Gerbils, hamsters, mice and rats are all rodents.
5. Joshua's uncle was rescued on February 27, 1977.

☆ **Something Extra**
Can you say the alphabet backwards? Give someone this page so they can see if you get it right.

z y x w v u t s r q p o n m l k j i h g f e d c b a

48

page 48

back

Finish the graph. Use separate lines for the high temperatures and the low temperatures.

	Sun.	Mon.	Tues.	Wed.	Thurs.	Fri.	Sat.
High	75	80	83	82	82	79	81
Low	69	71	70	70	68	69	69

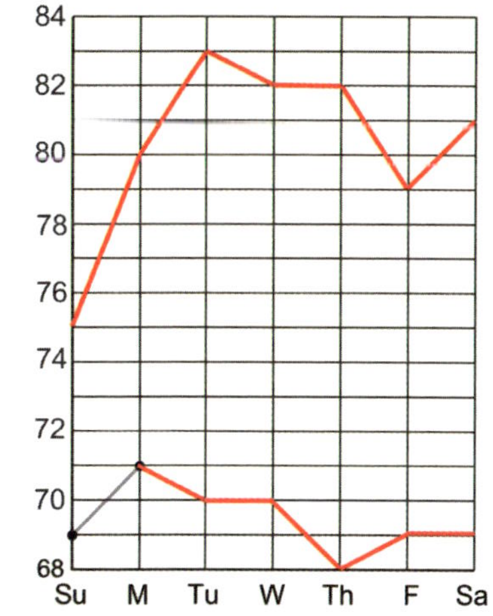

front

Thursday

Divide.

64 ÷ 8 = 8	25 ÷ 5 = 5	9 ÷ 3 = 3	12 ÷ 4 = 3
14 ÷ 2 = 7	18 ÷ 2 = 9	1 ÷ 1 = 1	36 ÷ 9 = 4
36 ÷ 4 = 9	48 ÷ 8 = 6	0 ÷ 5 = 0	21 ÷ 7 = 3

Add.

94	87	479	23	298	273	182	96
18	535	64	41	143	485	55	414
+ 59	+ 62	+ 76	+ 346	+ 517	+ 31	+ 348	+ 557
171	684	619	410	958	789	585	1,067

Choose three of the phrases below and use each of them in a complete sentence.

splashing each other — a shaggy dog — running as fast as he could — a tiny, little mouse — a long flowing streamer

Answers will vary.

Make the dark word plural and write it on the lines to make a good sentence.

penny 1. Jan has saved three quarters and six __pennies__.
foot 2. Do you know how many __feet__ a caterpillar has?
half 3. James very carefully cut the candy bars into __halves__.
woman 4. The __women__ in the choir all sang beautifully.
loaf 5. Mother baked five __loaves__ of bread yesterday.

49

page 49

back

Number each group of words in alphabetical order.

1 Saturday	4 size	3 shell	4 skate
3 selfish	1 sack	5 slurp	1 sardine
5 share	3 shiver	4 side	2 scope
2 scrap	5 skill	1 saw	3 seat
4 seven	2 seal	2 second	5 slim

Place a check mark in the correct box.

Word	Guide Words	Relation to the Page		
1. wise	wisdom - wonder	□ before	☑ on	□ after
2. ransom	redeem - review	☑ before	□ on	□ after
3. mouth	Michigan - missed	□ before	□ on	☑ after
4. bow	beau - breeze	□ before	☑ on	□ after
5. exalt	esteem - everlasting	□ before	□ on	☑ after
6. sword	skill - sorry	□ before	□ on	☑ after
7. prudent	patient - peculiar	□ before	□ on	☑ after
8. kind	keep - kitchen	□ before	☑ on	□ after
9. gate	genteel - gentle	☑ before	□ on	□ after
10. truth	tea - tulip	□ before	☑ on	□ after
11. ox	obey - peculiar	□ before	☑ on	□ after
12. understand	umbrella - violin	□ before	☑ on	□ after

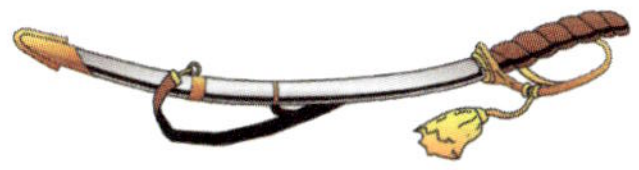

front

Friday

Write the numeral for these number words.

four thousand, three hundred sixty-five __4,365__
eight hundred thirteen thousand, nine hundred two __813,902__
sixty thousand, four hundred seventy __60,470__
seven million, twelve thousand, three __7,012,003__

Solve these story problems.

1. Mr. King has 31 children in his 4th grade class. 17 of them are boys, and 14 are girls. If 4 children were absent yesterday, how many were at school?
   31-4=27
2. Morgan took the bus downtown for \$0.75. Then he got on another bus to go to the park for a game of Frisbee with his friends. That cost \$0.35. How much will it cost him to go to the park and get back home?
   \$0.75+\$0.35=\$1.10 \$1.10x2=\$2.20

3. Bill is saving for a new Ultra-Frisbee which costs \$16. He earns \$5.50 a week mowing lawns. How many weeks will it take him to earn enough to buy the Ultra-Frisbee?
   3

*Tell whether the pairs of words are synonyms (**syn.**), antonyms (**ant.**) or homonyms (**hom.**).*

boy, girl __ant.__	car, automobile __syn.__	rain, reign __hom.__
sign, banner __syn.__	to, two __hom.__	heavy, light __ant.__
slay, sleigh __hom.__	young, old __ant.__	small, little __syn.__
truth, lie __ant.__	pop, soda __syn.__	scene, seen __hom.__

Write a letter to a relative whom you haven't seen recently. Tell them about what you have been doing this summer. Check your letter by the questions below. Then have an adult help you address the envelope and mail it.

___ Did you write neatly?
___ Did you use capital letters and periods?
___ Are all the words spelled correctly?

50

page 50

back

The Marmot
from *An Alphabet of Quadrupeds*

Marmots live in the Alps and other high mountains. They live right below the area that always has snow. They are about the size of a hare and are a yellowish green color. Marmots live in families. They work together to build the home. The room in which they live is lined with dried grass and is at the end of a passage. The passage is six or eight feet long and forms the letter Y. One of the branches is the entrance. The other is a sewer. During winter, the mouth of the passage is closed by earth. Marmots eat together, but they always have a guard. At the first sign of danger, the guard utters a shrill cry and the whole group leaves.

Answer the questions about the paragraph.

1. What is a sewer? __something that carries away waste__
2. What do marmots always have when they are eating? __a guard__
3. Marmots live on what kind of land? (mountain) valley plain
4. Marmots are most like the size of what animals? ants (raccoons) tigers
5. Draw a picture of the marmots' home based on the description in the paragraph.

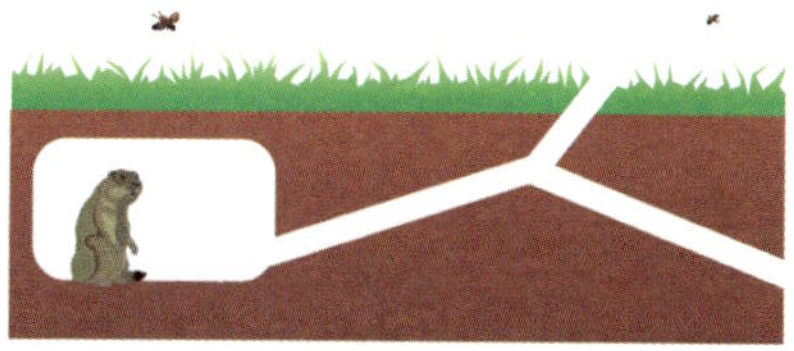

Know it all in the fall . . .

Summer Book K is for students entering kindergarten (K5). It contains fifty pages of daily work. The front of each page contains written activities for the child to complete. The back of each page suggests fun games and activities as well as tips for parents. A complete answer key is included.

Upper- and lower-case magnetic letters and numbers are included with the book as well as shapes in a wide variety of colors.

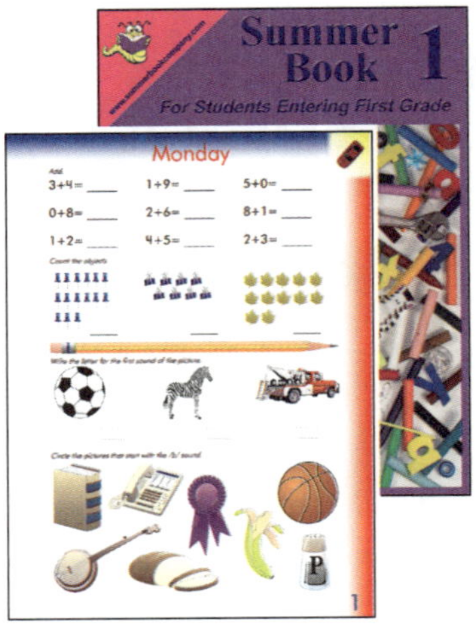

Summer Book 1 is for students entering first grade. Students will know it all in the fall by thoroughly reviewing reading, math, phonics and thinking skills. Fifty daily pages and answer key.

Special Fun: Develop visual tracking skills by playing "I spy" each day. The item of the day is on the top corner of the page and can be found on either the front or back cover of the book.

Summer Book 2 is for students entering second grade. Know it all in the fall by thoroughly reviewing math, reading comprehension, writing, phonics and thinking skills. Fifty daily pages and answer key.

Special Fun: Encourage patience, persistence, and visual skills while going through the maze on the back of each page.

Summer Book 3 is for students entering third grade. Students will know it all in the fall by thoroughly reviewing math, reading comprehension, writing, English and thinking skills. Fifty daily pages and answer key.

Special Fun: "Visit the zoo" all summer and learn about a different animal each day.

. . . with only one book!

Summer Book 4 is for students entering fourth grade. Contains fifty daily pages and an answer key.

Extras: Enjoy learning about many different sports and outdoor activities.

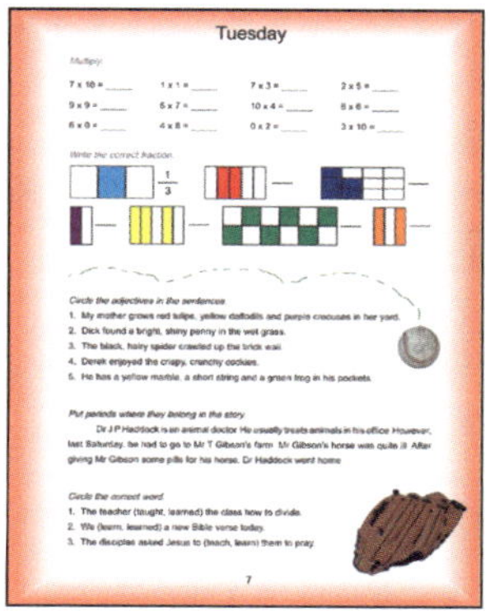

Summer Books 4-7 thoroughly review math, reading comprehension, grammar, writing, and thinking skills. History, health and science are also refreshed.

Summer Book 5 is for students entering fifth grade. Contains fifty daily pages and an answer key.

Extras: Learn about different rocks and beautiful gemstones (in the new edition in 2008). Also practice map skills and shopping wisdom.

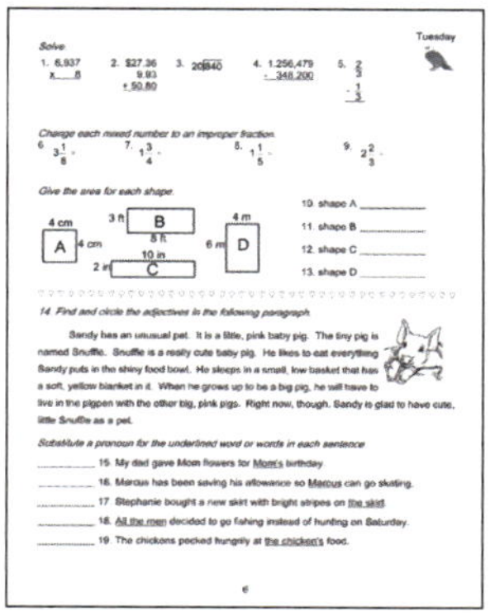

Summer Book 6 is for students entering sixth grade. Contains fifty daily pages and an answer key.

Extras: Discover outer space, planets, astronauts and trips to the moon.

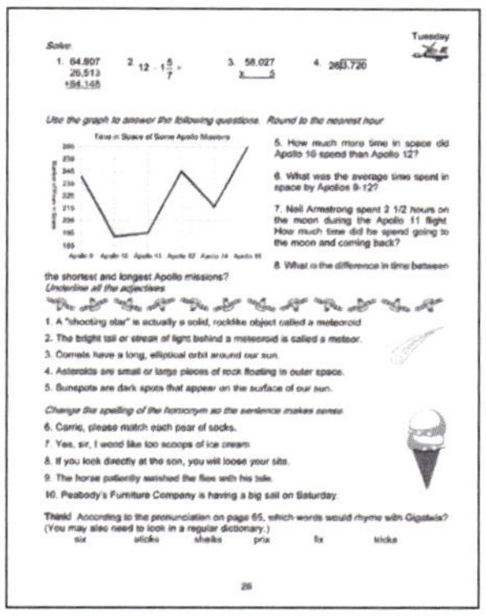

New color editions of
Summer Books 5, 6 and 7
coming in the spring of 2008

Summer Book 7 is for students entering seventh grade. Contains fifty daily pages and an answer key.

Extras: Improve world geography skills by learning about a new country each day and identifying it on the world map.

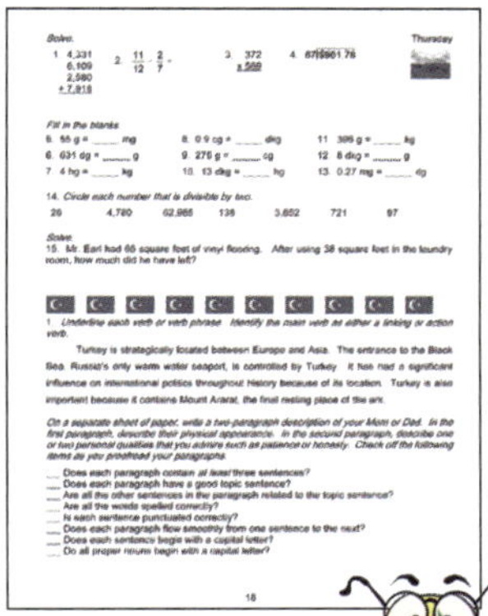

Reading Comprehension for Everyone

With bright, colorful pictures, the *Summerbook Readers* are a delight for beginners. The short-vowel words and short sentences help new readers gain confidence quickly. Paperback, 40 pages each. (set of 3) 62 free reproducible worksheets to accompany the books are available on-line. Grade K

Bible Stories for Early Readers Set of 5 books with The Dreams Come True, The Ten Lepers, Pigs You Stink, The Big Quake, And Joseph and His Coat. 32 pages each. Paperback. Comprehension questions at the back of each book. Grade 1

Bible Stories for Early Readers focuses on the two-vowel rule. Set of 5 books with God Adds Oil, Zacchaeus' Cash Bag, 3 Brave Men , 7 Dips, Jonah's Ride. Paperback, 32 pages each. Comprehension questions at the back of each book. Grade 1

Help your child answer fascinating questions with these simple books. Bright, full-page photographs help to make them a pleasure to read again and again. Paperback, 24 pages each. *Start to Finish* (set of 5) comes with comprehension questions and vocabulary puzzles. Grade 2

Each book comes with comprehension questions and vocabulary puzzles.
More free materials and additional books are available at our website.

This over-sized book with glowing illustrations is sure to capture a child's heart. *The Legend of the Teddy Bear* tells the true story of how the first "Teddy's Bear" was created. Hardback, 32 pages. Grades K-3

A boy's delight! With *Bug Hunter* he will learn to catch and identify bugs and quickly complete the insect collection for school. Unfold identification charts inside the front and back covers. Paperback, 72 pages. Grades 3+

In *The Land Beyond the Setting Sun* learn how Sacagewea courageously aided in the explorations of Lewis and Clark. Captivating for a first biography. 60 pages, hardback. Grades 3+

Our Flag Was Still There! History is definitely not boring in this beautifully illustrated, action-packed retelling of the writing of our national anthem. Hardback, 44 pages. Grades 3+

In *Unfading Beauty* meet Dolley Madison, a truly gracious and brave First Lady. Fascinating for a first biography. Hardback, 60 pages. Grades 3+

Destination Moon is an intriguing travel with Colonel Irwin to the moon. Join him as he drives the first moon car. A great book for boys (and girls, too)! Stunning photographs. 64 pages, hardback. Grades 4+

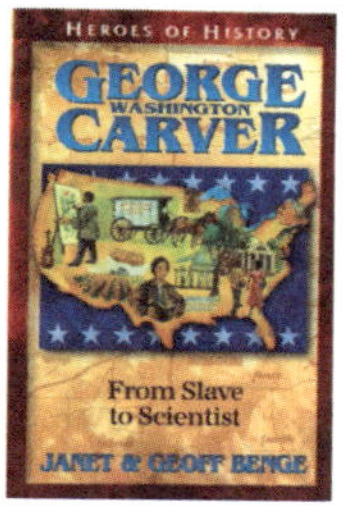

George Washington Carver After the Civil War, life was hard and racial tensions were high. Read the amazing story of a most resourceful man who helped to forever change the history of the South. Paperback, 189 pages. Grades 5+

Harriet Tubman She was wanted, dead or alive, and there were many who would have preferred her dead. However, she never quit risking her life to save the lives of others. Paperback, 191 pages. Grades 5+

Additional biographies in this series are available at our website.

Lillian Trasher An American woman taking care of thousands of orphans in Egypt all by herself? Sometimes truth is more amazing than fiction. Paperback, 229 pages. Grades 5+

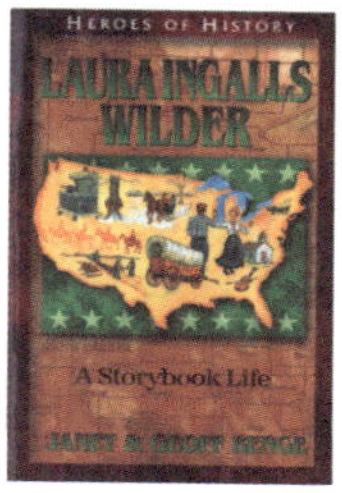

Laura Ingalls Wilder A pioneer, teacher, farmer's wife, and storyteller, Laura Ingalls Wilder experienced one of the most exciting times in American history - history she brought to life for millions. Paperback, 193 pages. Grades 5+

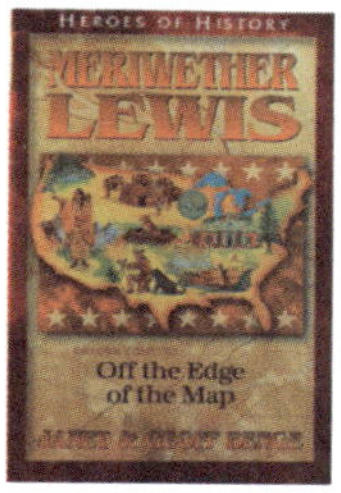

Merriwether Lewis The President gave him an almost impossible assignment: to boldly go where no explorer had gone before, cross the continent to the Pacific Ocean, and give a full report of the land. Paperback, 229 pages. Grades 6+

Barbara and Regina held firmly to the belief that they were *Alone, yet not Alone*, even when they had been captured by Indians and taken far from their parents. A true story. Hardback, 200 pages. Grades 6+

☞ English grammar made easy . . . finally! ☜

Step-by-Step Grammar Volume I: Basic Grammar teaches the basic eight parts of speech. It also teaches diagraming, compound sentences, prepositional phrases, and verb phrases. This book is written to be used by fifth and sixth graders who are struggling with grammar. *However, anyone who lacks a solid understanding of the basic eight parts of speech will benefit from this approach.* 119 pages. Grades 4+

Grammar Study Cards help students memorize basic definitions and lists.

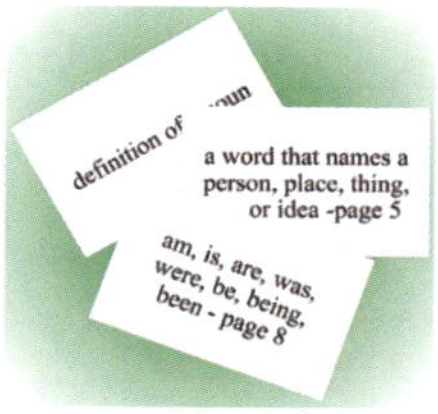

To see sample pages or download other free pages, visit our website, www.summerbookcompany.com.

Step-by-Step Grammar Volume II: Basic Usage was written to go with *Volume I: Basic Grammar* but can be used independently. This second book teaches punctuation usage, subject-verb agreement, plurals, possessive forms and other sentence necessities. It helps your child understand the rules for written English and learn how to put a sentence together properly and punctuate it correctly. 190 pages. Grades 4+

Bend your brain and THINK

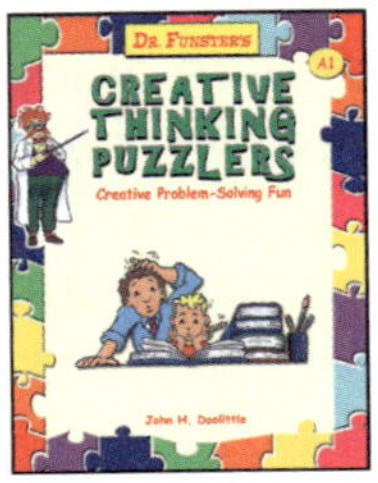

Creative Thinking Puzzlers A variety of puzzles to stretch the brain and encourage thinking. 45 pages. Answer key included.

Grades 3-5	#TCPA
Grades 6-8	#TCPB
Grades 9-12	#TCPC

Think Analogies Fantastic preparation for achievement tests. 50-60 pages. Answer key included.

Grades 3-5	#TAA1
Grades 6-8	#TAB1

All books on this page are REPRODUCIBLE.

Think-A-Minutes Engaging puzzles to wake up the mind and spark creativity. 45 pages. Answer key included.

Grades 2-3	#TMA1
Grades 2-3	#TMA2
Grades 4-5	#TMB1
Grades 4-5	#TMB2
Grades 6-8	#TMC1

Mind Benders These deductive thinking puzzles develop reading comprehension, logic, and mental organization. Answer key included. 40-59 pages.

Grade PreK-K	#TBE1
Grades 1-2	#TBE2
Grades 3-6	#TBA1
Grades 7-12	#TBB1

Word Benders Build spelling, vocabulary and comprehension. 30 pages. Answer key included.

Grades 3-5	#TEA1
Grades 6-8	#TEB2

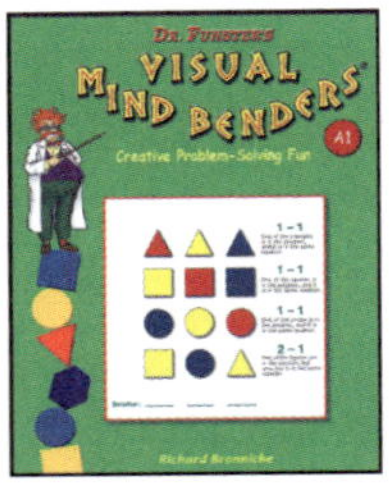

Visual Mind Benders Analyze the shapes, develop new thinking skills, solve the puzzle. 30 pages. Answer key included.

Grades 4-6	#TVA1
Grades 7-9	#TVB1
Grades 10-12	#TVC1

Building Thinking Skills

This exceptional skill set provides a solid foundation for academic excellence and success on any assessment test. 600+ pages.

Level 1	Grades 2-3	#TS1S
Level 2	Grades 4-6	#TS2S

Student books 250+ pages. Separate answer key with lesson plans. 270+ pages each.

Level 3 - Verbal	Grades 7-12	#TS3S
Level 3 - Verbal.-Ans.	Grades 7-12	#TSVA
Level 3 - Figural	Grades 7-12	#TSFS
Level 3 - Fig.-Ans.	Grades 7-12	#TSFA

Take the sting out of story problems

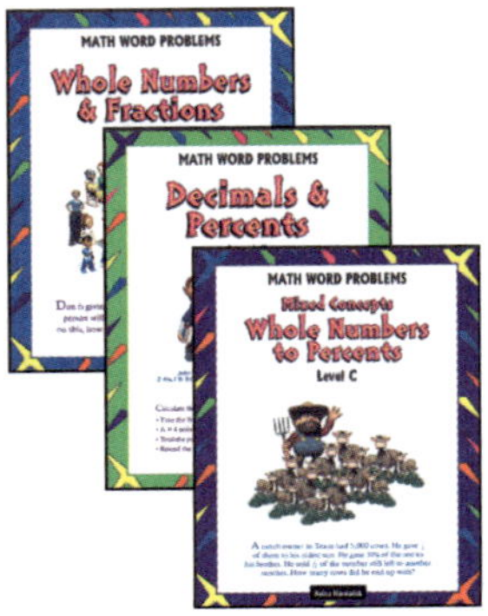

Whole Numbers & Fractions A	Grades 4-6	#TWPA
Decimals & Percents B	Grades 5-8	#TWPB
Whole Num. to Percents C	Grades 5-10	#TWPC
Algebra I Word Problems	Grades 7-12	#TWA1
Algebra II Word Problems	Grades 7-12	#TWA2
Scratch Your Brain Geometry	Grades 8-12	#TWSG

Master the Basics

Children need lots of drill on the basic math facts to truly master them. These **reproducible** books will help make it easy for you to give your child all the drill he or she needs.

The Basic Facts Drill Book for Addition and Subtraction drills 0+0 through 9+9 and the corresponding subtraction problems. 120 pages.

The Basic Facts Drill Book for Multiplication and Division drills 0x0 through 12x12 and the corresponding division problems. 120 pages.

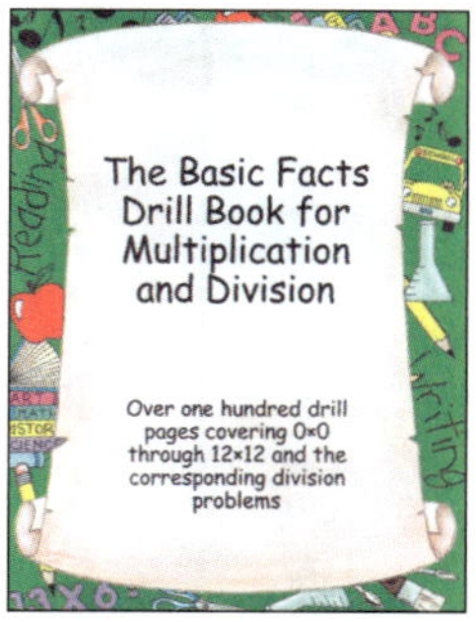

Spelling, Phonics and Parenting

Reading Through Spelling will help you as a parent teach your child to read by helping your child become a good speller. 41 pages.

Supplementary Phonics Tips If your child is using the *A Beka* curriculum, and the phonics has you worried, this booklet is for you. 24 pages.

To Train Up A Child From successful parents, learn how to bring joy and peace into your home. The emphasis is on training a child before the need to discipline arises. 122 pages.

Play and Learn with Educational Dice

LCR Have loads of fun learning the difference between left and right. Even adults enjoy this one! Grade PreK+

Double Dice Dice inside dice! Unique dice make this scoring and calculating game twice the fun. Grade 3+

Dinosaurs Don't get eaten by a T. rex while counting and adding. Simple and advanced directions included. Grade K+

Fraction Pack Take the fear out of fractions. Suggestions for parents included. Grade 4+

Trains Build the best train in three rolls. Simple and advanced directions included. Grade K+

Word Rally A great spelling game to take in your pocket. Children and adults can play together. Grade 1+

Bearly There While adding to 49, don't be "unbearable." Two other games included. Grade 2+

We also have various individual dice. For information and ideas, visit www.summerbookcompany.com.

Brain Bender Can you add, multiply, subtract and divide fast enough to win? Grade 4+

Help! My child is having trouble in school. He . . .

is having trouble learning to read.

The Knowledge Nurse recommends:
Reading Through Spelling, page C6
Summerbook Readers, page C3
Supplementary Phonics Tips, page C6

doesn't remember what he has read.

The Knowledge Nurse recommends:
an appropriate book from page C3
and reading the tip page on the website about reading comprehension

really hates to read.

The Knowledge Nurse recommends:
an appropriate book from page C3
and reading the tip page on the website about reading comprehension

has just terrible spelling.

The Knowledge Nurse recommends:
Reading Through Spelling, page C6
Supplementary Phonics Tips, page C6

is doing poorly in English.

The Knowledge Nurse recommends:
Step-by-Step Grammar, page C4

doesn't know his basic math facts.

The Knowledge Nurse recommends:
The Basic Math Facts books, page C6
Dice games, page C6

has real trouble with math story problems.

The Knowledge Nurse recommends:
an appropriate book from page C5

is generally behind everyone else in his class.

The Knowledge Nurse recommends:
a *Summer Book* from page C1 or C2

just does not think.

The Knowledge Nurse recommends:
a Thinking Skills book from page C5

More help is available on the web at www.summerbookcompany.com, or you can speak to a "knowledge nurse" toll free at 877-684-8502.

My child is doing well in school. I need something to challenge him. What do you recommend?

1. Your child would probably enjoy the puzzles in the Thinking Skills books on page C5, especially the thick *Building Thinking Skills*.
2. Have your child read books that are a little harder by choosing books from page C2 that are a grade or two above his current level. The website has additional books from which to choose.
3. Get a dice game from page C7 for variety and a challenge.